Excel 2000
An Advanced Course for Students

P. D'Larselle

Dec. 02

Excel 2000
An Advanced
Course for
Students

Jim Muir

Senior Lecturer in Business Computing

Bournemouth University

Learning Matters

First published in 2000 by Learning Matters Ltd.
Reprinted in 2001.

British Library Cataloguing in Publication Data
A CIP record for this book is available from the British Library.

ISBN 1 903300 17 7

Cover and text design by Code 5 Design Associates Ltd
Project management by Deer Park Productions
Typeset by PDQ Typesetting
Printed and bound in Great Britain by The Baskerville Press Ltd, Salisbury, Wiltshire.

Learning Matters Ltd
58 Wonford Road
Exeter EX2 4LQ
Tel: 01392 215560
Email: info@learningmatters.co.uk
www.learningmatters.co.uk

Contents

v

Other titles in this series

This is one of a series of course books for students, covering the three major components of the Microsoft Office 2000 suite of software.

Access 2000
An Introductory Course for Students
Sue Coles and Jenny Rowley
ISBN 1 903300 14 2

Access 2000
An Advanced Course for Students
Sue Coles and Jenny Rowley
ISBN 1 903300 15 0

Excel 2000
An Introductory Course for Students
Jim Muir
ISBN 1 903300 16 9

Excel 2000
An Advanced Course for Students
Jim Muir
ISBN 1 903300 17 7

Word 2000
An Introductory Course for Students
Sue Coles and Jenny Rowley
ISBN 1 903300 18 5

Word 2000
An Advanced Course for Students
Sue Coles and Jenny Rowley
ISBN 1 903300 19 3

To order, please contact our distributors:
Plymbridge Distributors, Estover Road, Plymouth, PL6 7PY.
Tel: 01752 202301   Fax: 01752 202333   Email: orders@plymbridge.com

Learning with this book

This book introduces Excel 2000, the latest version of Microsoft's Excel spreadsheet software. Excel is a component of the Office 2000 suite of application software, which also includes Access, Word and PowerPoint. Data can be easily transferred between these different applications.

The book is designed for anyone who wants to learn how to use Excel. This includes students in further and higher education, as well as professional users. Students who might benefit from this book are likely to be learning spreadsheets as part of an accounting, business studies, social sciences, information systems, management studies, or marketing course. It has been written for people who already have some working knowledge of Excel, and can create and manipulate spreadsheets, produce charts and use databases. However it includes some elementary and intermediate material as a way of filling in any gaps in readers' background knowledge.

Approach

The underlying philosophy of this book is concerned with learning by doing. It focuses on tasks and activities, and in every Topic the pace of presentation is lively and you will not be burdened unduly by blow by blow descriptions of keystrokes and mouse movements.

The book is divided into 13 Topics, each one taking about one hour to complete. Each Topic is based around one or two straightforward examples. Unless you need to refresh some of your elementary and intermediate skills, there is no necessity to work through the Topics in sequence. Occasionally you may be recommended to use a workbook created in an earlier unit, but this is not essential. A number of independent tasks have also been included for you to try. The general approach is that a workbook seldom remains fixed, there are always ways in which it can be modified or extended. The Excel screen shots provided will help you check your learning at key stages.

Excel 2000 incorporates a number of new features which are covered in this book. These include:

PivotChart Reports

Web Queries

Excel-based Web Pages

Short and Full Menus

Features in the text

The following features have been used throughout the book to make the practical instructions clear:

1. Bold capitals indicate a feature from the screen, for example **BUTTON** or **DIALOG BOX NAME**.
   Menu instructions are also presented this way: **EDIT-COPY** means choose **COPY** from the **EDIT** menu.

2. White bold capitals in a panel indicate the names of keys on the keyboard, for example **ESC** or **F1**.

3. Bold text in upper and lower case indicates names of **Fields**, **Tables**, **Queries**, **Forms** and **Reports**.

4. Italic text on a shaded background indicates *Text to be keyed in* .

Online Copies of the Workbooks

The final versions of the Excel workbooks created in this book can be obtained free of charge from the publisher's website **www.learningmatters.co.uk**.

Worksheet Basics

Introduction

The overall appearance of the Excel screen has changed little in recent versions (from Excel 7 onwards) so I have kept the introductory parts of this first topic fairly brief; if you already have a working familiarity with Excel I suggest that you 'skim' the tasks in this topic. Create the workbook **Budget** along the lines suggested as we shall be using it in later topics.

Topic Objectives

- To review the components of the Excel window.
- To enter and amend worksheet data.
- To adjust the dimensions of columns and rows.
- To make simple calculations using formulae.
- To close and open a workbook.
- To copy data using Paste, Fill and AutoFill commands.
- To use Excel Help and Office Assistant.

The Excel Screen – an Overview

1 Before we begin take a few minutes to identify the following Excel features shown in Figure 1.1.

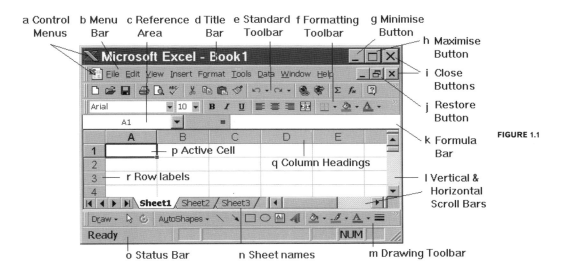

FIGURE 1.1

2 (a) **The Control Menu Boxes** let you close or vary the size of the window.

(b) **The Menu Bar** offers the usual options – File, Edit, View etc.

(c) **The Reference Area** confirms which cell in the worksheet is active – see section p below.

(d) **The Title Bar** shows the name of the workbook currently in use; if it has not been saved yet it shows a default name, Book1, Book2 etc.

(e) and (f) **The Tool Bars**. The **Standard Toolbar** and the **Formatting Toolbar** offer alternative ways of issuing commands to the menus, eg opening and saving files, copying, printing, formatting etc. You can hide or display toolbars by using the **VIEW-TOOLBARS** menu options.

(g)–(j) To control the size of the window are buttons (g)–(j) – features of all Windows applications. You may see two sets, one to control the inner worksheet document, and one for the overall application.

(g) **The Minimise Button** (shown as a line).

(h) **The Maximise Button** (shown as a square).

(i) **The Close Button** (shown as an 'X').

(j) **The Restore Button** (shown as overlapping squares).

(k) **The Formula Bar** will display the contents of whatever cell is currently selected – the 'active' cell. Use the **TOOLS-VIEW** menu to display the Formula Bar if necessary.

(l) **The Horizontal and Vertical Scroll Bars**.

(m) **The Drawing Toolbar** may be displayed. You can use it to add standard shapes to your worksheet, as well as altering text style and colour effects.

(n) **Sheet Names**. The name tab of the active sheet is shown in bold – Sheet 1 at the moment.

(o) **The Status Bar** shows the progress of any commands, operations etc currently being executed; it displays a 'Ready' message when no commands etc are executing.

(p) **The Active Cell** is the cell currently in use, identified by a heavy border.

(q) **Column Headings** and (r) **Row Labels** combined give the cell reference or address.

3 The sections that follow try out some of these Excel components; skip them if you know them already.

4 **Minimising the Excel Window**. Click the topmost **MINIMISE** button and Excel shrinks to a button on the Windows Taskbar. Click this button to restore the Excel window.

5 *Note*: Remember that pressing the **ALT** and the **TAB** keys together will review all the applications that are running, so if you can't see the Excel button you can restore the Excel window this way.

6 **Maximising and Restoring the Excel Window**. Try this for both the inner worksheet document and for the outer application window.

(7) **Changing the Window Size**. All windows can be re-sized by dragging them – try this, remembering that it will not work if the window is maximised.

(8) **Moving an Excel Window**. Similarly drag the Title Bar of the inner and outer windows – they can be moved independently, provided again that they are not maximised.

(9) **Using the Keyboard**. Try these keyboard shortcuts – they are quicker than using the scrollbars in many instances.

(a) Press the **CTRL** and **HOME** keys – you are taken to cell A1.

(b) Press the **CTRL** and **DOWN ARROW** keys – you go to row 65536, the last row in the worksheet. If your worksheet contains data then you will go to the last row containing data.

(c) Press the **CTRL** and the **RIGHT ARROW** key – you go to the last column in the worksheet.

(d) Now experiment with **CTRL - LEFT ARROW** and **CTRL - RIGHT ARROW** Try out the **PAGE UP** and **PAGE DOWN** keys too.

(10) **Selecting Cell Ranges**. Try dragging the mouse to select the following ranges or groups of cells:

(a) Select cell range **A1** to **D6**; 24 cells are selected or 'highlighted' but **A1** remains the active cell, even though all the column and row designators in the range change to bold – A-D and 1-6.

(b) Clicking outside this range de-selects it; click the column designator for column A and the whole column is selected. Drag across several column designators to select several columns.

(11) **Using Excel Help**. Each version of Excel adds extra features so try out the following options:
Open the **HELP** menu and select **MICROSOFT EXCEL HELP**; if the 'Office Assistant' logo – an animated paperclip – appears you can turn it off as explained below.
Three tabs are shown – **CONTENT, ANSWER WIZARD** and **INDEX**.

Note: **The Office Assistant**. This feature can be irritating to more advanced learners. To turn it off permanently click the **OPTIONS** button on the Office Assistant dialog box and de-select the **USE THE OFFICE ASSISTANT** check box.

(12) **Help Contents**. Select the **CONTENTS** tab. In the left-hand side of the window the help topics are depicted as chapters in a book.
Select the topic **GETTING HELP**. The book icon opens showing a series of subtopics.
Read a few of these subtopics; the text on the right of the window changes with the topic.

(13) **The Help Index**. Click the **INDEX** tab. Help topics are listed in the left-hand side of the window. Scroll down to the topic **MENU** and select it. Click the **SEARCH** button and a number of relevant Help topics are displayed.

(14) **Keying in a Help Topic**. Instead of scrolling through the topic list you can type in the Help topic you want. First clear any keywords from the text box and enter the topic *worksheet*. Press the **ENTER** key and the topic is displayed.

(15) **Answer Wizard**. Excel Help offers this third option by answering questions typed in ordinary English.Take some time to explore it.

(16) **The 'What's This?'** option identifies and explains particular Excel features. Close Help then select this option from the main Help menu. Every time the screen pointer changes to a '?' shape you can click on an Excel object and get help on it.

(17) **Help on Tool Bars**. Rest the screen pointer on top of a button and its purpose is described.

Entering Worksheet Data

(1) We are now ready to create our first worksheet, based around a student's personal finances – see Figure 1.2. Later on I shall be asking you to modify it but at the moment create it exactly as shown. Make sure that you enter the number 0 and not the letter O (a common source of error). *Don't calculate the worksheet totals yet*.

FIGURE 1.2

	A	B	C	D	E
1			Finances - Spring Term		
2					
3	INCOME		Week 1		
4	Starting Bals		80		
5	Loan		900		
6	Part-time job		55		
7	Total Income				
8					
9	OUTGOINGS				
10	Accomodation		65		
11	Food		40		
12	Books		60		
13	Social		30		
14	Total Outgoings				
15					

2 **Cell Titles and Labels**. Create the worksheet shown in Figure 1.2. Remember that although the data is shown in the Formula Bar as you type, the cell's contents are not finally entered until you click the 'tick' box in the Formula Bar or press the **ENTER** key. Selecting another cell in the workbook has the same effect. If you forget to complete a cell entry you may find that various Excel features no longer work, eg menu options. When you enter the word **Accomodation** be sure to spell it incorrectly as I have done – see next section!

3 **Excel's Spell Checker**. We will start checking from the beginning of the worksheet so select cell **A1**. Click the **SPELLING** button – on the Standard Toolbar, marked 'ABC'. A dialog box will identify 'Bals' as not in the dictionary – click the **IGNORE** button. **Accomodation** is identified as misspelt; use the **CHANGE** button to select the correct spelling.

Note: You can add valid words, eg names, acronyms etc, to the spell checker dictionary using the **ADD** button.

4 **AutoCorrect**. This feature will automatically correct misspelt words as you type. If you want to use it select it from the **TOOLS** menu. If the option appears to be missing then follow the instructions in the note below.

Note: Short and Full Menu options are a new Excel 2000 feature; we will be using Full menus so open the **TOOLS** menu and select **CUSTOMISE**. Click the **OPTIONS** tab and de-select the option **MENUS SHOW RECENTLY USED COMMANDS FIRST**.

5 **Amending an Entry Using the Formula Bar**. To alter the text in cell A5 from Loan to Student Loan first select the cell.
Now click in front of the first letter of **Loan** in the Formula Bar and the pointer shape becomes a flashing cursor marking the insertion point – see Figure 1.3.
You can now amend the cell.

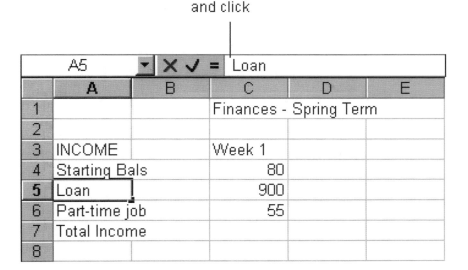

locate cursor here
and click

FIGURE 1.3

(6) **In-Cell Editing**. Let's alter the label *Food* in cell A11 to *Food and Travel* directly without using the Formula Bar. Double click the space after the word *Food* and the flashing cursor marks the insertion point.

Note: Deleting and Overtyping. You can use the `DELETE` and `BACKSPACE` keys in the usual ways; remember that you can delete the contents of a cell directly by overtyping – there is no need to delete them first.

(7) **Widening Columns**. Try out these three ways on column A:

(a) **Dragging**. Place the screen pointer on column designator A; move it until it covers the vertical line separating it from column B – the pointer is now a double-headed arrow.
Simply drag right until it is about 16.00 wide.

(b) Select a cell in column A then take the menu options **FORMAT-COLUMN-WIDTH**. Set it to 15.00.

(c) Repeat step (b) but this time select the options **FORMAT-COLUMN-AUTOFIT SELECTION**. The column is adjusted to fit the entry in the cell selected.

(8) **Altering Row Height**. Use the same techniques to make row 1 higher – about 16.00.

(9) **Optional – Saving the Workbook**: If you are not proceeding to the next task then save and close the workbook. Give it the name **Budget**. Saving involves the usual steps of selecting a suitable drive/folder for this and the rest of your Excel work.

Entering Formulae

All Excel calculations involve formulae which must begin with an = sign. Later in the book we will be using complex formulae involving functions and external references to other workbooks.

(1) **Addition**. We need to total income and outogings for the first week of the spring term – see Figure 1.2 above. Select cell **C7** and enter the formula **=SUM(C4:C6)** in upper or lower case. Total income is now displayed in the cell.
Note that using the SUM function is quicker than using the '+' sign, eg =C4+C5+C6. Another big advantage of using the SUM function is expandability – the formula is automatically adjusted if another row is inserted into the column of cells.

(2) **Adding Up Columns by Dragging**. To total up the Outgoings enter **=SUM(** in cell C14.
Now use the screen pointer to select cell range **C10** to **C13** – they are enclosed in a dotted box. The Formula Bar shows the range selected.
If correct click the 'tick' box or press `ENTER` and the result of the formula is displayed in cell C14.

(3) **Formula Error Messages**. Try out the following:

Select cell **C7** and then click the formula displayed in the Formula Bar – the Excel Range Finder feature highlights the relevant cells in colour.
If you amend the formula to =SUM(C4:**C7**) an Excel error message tells you that the reference is 'circular' – as C7 is the destination cell for the formula it cannot also be one of the cells included in the formula. Click the **CANCEL** button and correct the formula to =SUM(C4:C6)

(4) We'll look at one more of Excel's many error messages. Select cell **C14** and amend the spelling of SUM to SIM. The error message *#NAME?* alerts you to this.
Clear the contents of cell C14 using either the ■DELETE■ key or the menu options **EDIT-CLEAR-ALL**.

(5) **Using AutoSum**. The AutoSum button is marked with the Greek character Sigma (Σ). Select cell **C14** then click the AutoSum button – it is on the Standard Toolbar.
The correct cell range should be selected; click the AutoSum button again.

Note: Use AutoSum with care – you cannot rely on it always to select the correct range of cells.

(6) **AutoCalculate**. This feature will automatically display the sum of any group of numeric cells that you select at the bottom right of the window. It is for information, however, and will not execute without a formula being entered.

(7) **Subtraction**. Figure 1.4 below shows where we have reached in our worksheet, with the exception of the balance figure which we will now calculate.
Enter the formula =**C7-C14** in cell **C16** to find the closing balance for week1.

	A	B	C	D	E
1			Finances - Spring Term		
2					
3	INCOME		Week 1		
4	Starting Bals		80		
5	Student Loan		900		
6	Part-time job		55		
7	Total Income		1035		
8					
9	OUTGOINGS				
10	Accommodation		65		
11	Food and Travel		40		
12	Books		60		
13	Social		30		
14	Total Outgoings		195		
15					
16	Closing Balance		840		
17					

FIGURE 1.4

7

Saving and Opening a Workbook (Optional)

At this point save the workbook; give it the name **Budget** if you have not saved it yet. Saving involves the usual steps of selecting a suitable drive/folder for this workbook and the rest of your Excel work. Refer to the notes below if you need to:

① Use the menu options **FILE-SAVE AS** to save a new workbook for the first time. Use **FILE-SAVE** to save changes to an existing workbook.

② New workbooks have the default name Book1, Book2 etc.

③ .XLS is the standard file extension assigned to Excel workbook files, normally you never need to change this.

④ A filename can be up to 218 characters long; it can consist of any combination of letters, numbers and certain special characters including spaces, dashes and underscores but not the following: \ / < > * ? " ; or :

⑤ **Closing and Exiting**. The **FILE-EXIT** option closes the whole Excel application; you will be prompted to save and close any open workbooks. The **FILE-CLOSE** option closes the workbook currently in use.

⑥ **Opening a Workbook**. In the **FILE-OPEN** dialog box you can simply type the name and folder in the **FILE NAME** box or you can open a workbook by choosing it from a list in the **LOOK IN**: box. Excel also remembers the last 4 workbooks that you (or another user of the application) have used. You can see them listed when you open the File menu.

Copying and Deleting

In this task we will review different ways to move, copy, and delete cells and extend our workbook to cover more weeks.

① **Copying**. Select cell range **C3** to **C16** containing the items for week 1. Use the menu options **EDIT-COPY** – the area is selected.

② **Pasting**. Select cell **D3** next – this is the cell where the copied cells are to be pasted; you only need to indicate where the pasting will start, not the complete range. Use the menu options **EDIT-PASTE** – the cells are now copied. Notice that the original cells are still selected with a dotted line and could be pasted as many times as you wish. Press the **ESC** key to remove the selection.

Note: Copied cells are placed in a temporary holding area called the Clipboard. They remain there until some other Copy or Cut command overwrites them. Excel lets you Undo up to 16 actions using the **EDIT-UNDO** command.

③ Check on the copied cells D7, D14 and D16 - the formulae as well as the cell values have been copied; the references have been automatically amended to reflect their new position in column D. Such formulae are therefore said to contain *relative references*.

④ **Cutting and Pasting**. Cutting is similar to copying except that the cells are

removed from their original position; we will try this:
Select cells **D3** to **D16** and issue the **EDIT-CUT** command.
Select cell **E3** then issue the **EDIT-PASTE** command – the column is moved from column D to column E.

Note: If you prefer use the Cut, Copy and Paste tools on the Tool Bar instead.

5   **Clearing Cells**. Re-select the cell range **E3** to **E16** if necessary then issue the command **EDIT-CLEAR-ALL**.

6   **Using Fill Right**. Filling right is often superior to Edit-Copy when copying columns. Select the cell range **C3** to **C16** and, keeping the mouse button pressed down, drag across to the next column.
Compare the result to Figure 1.5 – the same range of cells should be selected in each column.

FIGURE 1.5

9

7   Issue the command **EDIT-FILL-RIGHT** and the cell range is copied into column D – you can use the **EDIT-UNDO** command to reverse it if it is incorrect.

Amend the label in cell **D3** to *Week 2*.

8   Delete the values from cells **D4** and **D5** – these items only apply to week 1. The column D totals are re-calculated. We now need to carry forward the closing balance from week 1 to the opening balance of week 2 to see the true financial position.
Select cell **D4** and enter the formula **=C16** – your closing balance for week 2 is now 700.

9   Now make the following changes to week 2:

Food and Travel 30
Books   10

The closing balance is now 760.

10   We can now complete weeks 3 to 5. Select the entries for week 2 – cells **D3** to **D16** – and drag across to columns E, F and G.

Cells **D3** to **G16** are now selected. Issue the command **EDIT-FILL-RIGHT** and your worksheet should resemble Figure 1.6. Remember to save your changes.

FIGURE 1.6

	A	B	C	D	E	F	G
1			Finances - Spring Term				
2							
3	INCOME		Week 1	Week 2	Week 2	Week 2	Week 2
4	Starting Bals		80	840	760	680	600
5	Student Loan		900				
6	Part-time job		55	55	55	55	55
7	Total Income		1035	895	815	735	655
8							
9	OUTGOINGS						
10	Accommodation		65	65	65	65	65
11	Food and Travel		40	30	30	30	30
12	Books		60	10	10	10	10
13	Social		30	30	30	30	30
14	Total Outgoings		195	135	135	135	135
15							
16	Closing Balance		840	760	680	600	520
17							

11 **Completing a Series using AutoFill.** Select cell **D3** and identify the small 'handle' at the bottom right-hand corner – see Figure 1.7. Carefully locate the mouse pointer on this handle – it becomes cross-shaped – and drag across to select cells **E3** to **G3.**
The cells should be labelled with the correct week numbers.

FIGURE 1.7

autofill handle

12 Save and close the workbook at this point if you are not carrying on with the next topic.

Printing, Formatting and Copying Your Worksheet

Introduction

In this topic we review the familiar areas of formatting, printing and copying and also cover AutoFormat, conditional formatting and copying and deleting worksheets. We also look at relative and absolute references and try out some independent activities. We will use the Budget workbook to practise with; if you use another one then the cell references will be different.

Topic Objectives

- To review the basics of worksheet formatting, drawing objects and printing.
- To practise copying, renaming and deleting worksheets.
- To calculate and format averages and percentages.
- To apply absolute references in formulae.
- To use AutoFormatting and Conditional Formatting.

Formatting the Worksheet

We will format the workbook **Budget**, created in the first Topic so that it resembles Figure 2.1. Open it if necessary.

	A	B	C	D	E	F
1			Finances - Spring Term			
2						
3	INCOME	Week 1	Week 2	Week 3	Week 4	Week 5
4	Starting Bals	£ 80.00	£840.00	£760.00	£680.00	£600.00
5	Student Loan	£ 900.00				
6	Part-time job	£ 55.00	£ 55.00	£ 55.00	£ 55.00	£ 55.00
7	Total Income	£1,035.00	£895.00	£815.00	£735.00	£655.00
8						
9	OUTGOINGS					
10	Accommodation	£ 65.00	£ 65.00	£ 65.00	£ 65.00	£ 65.00
11	Food and Travel	£ 40.00	£ 30.00	£ 30.00	£ 30.00	£ 30.00
12	Books	£ 60.00	£ 10.00	£ 10.00	£ 10.00	£ 10.00
13	Social	£ 30.00	£ 30.00	£ 30.00	£ 30.00	£ 30.00
14	Total Outgoings	£ 195.00	£135.00	£135.00	£135.00	£135.00
15						
16						
17	Closing Balance	£ 840.00	£760.00	£680.00	£600.00	£520.00

FIGURE 2.1

1   **Emboldening**. First put the worksheet title in bold – select it and click the **BOLD** button on the Formatting Toolbar (`CTRL-B` is a useful keyboard shortcut). Now embolden the row labels in column A and the week numbers in columns B to F, plus the end of week balances.

2   **Fonts**. We will reduce the size of the text in column A from the default of 10 to 8. Select the row labels in column A and click the down arrow next to the font size button – see Figure 2.2. You can also select a different font to Arial, the default.

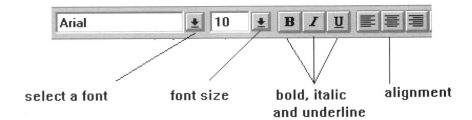

FIGURE 2.2

select a font   font size   bold, italic   alignment
and underline

3   **Alignment.** Excel automatically aligns numbers to the right of the cell, but they may look better centred under the column headings; Figure 2.2 shows the 3 alignment buttons. Select the numeric data and centre it.

4   **Number and Currency Formats.** Select all the numeric data again and choose the menu commands **FORMAT-CELLS-NUMBER**. Select **ACCOUNTING** then 2 decimal places. You may also need to choose the £ symbol. The cells should now display £ signs, requiring the column widths to be adjusted.

Note: To use a currency symbol in Excel (eg pound, dollar or Euro sign) you must use formatting; never type it in yourself or Excel will not treat the figures as numbers but as text, causing errors in calculations.

5   **Columns and Rows – Deleting and Inserting**. As column B is blank at the moment it can be removed without affecting any data and formulae. Delete it by first clicking the column designator (the 'B') then using the **EDIT-DELETE** menu commands. The remaining columns automatically shift to the left and any formulae are automatically amended to take account of their new position.
Insert a new row above row 15 using the **INSERT-ROWS** command.

6   **Centring Across Cells.** In Figure 2.2 we have centred the title across columns A to F. To do this first select cell range **A1** to **F1** then click the **MERGE AND CENTRE** button on the Formatting Toolbar (marked with a small 'a' and 2 arrows).

Note: The merge and centre feature in effect merges the 5 cells into one so they can no longer be individually selected. If this becomes a problem then right-click the merged cells and take the options **FORMAT-CELLS-ALIGNMENT**. You can then de-select the merged cells box.

7   **Lines and Borders**. You will notice that the worksheet in Figure 2.1 is divided into sections using borders. First select the entire worksheet, ie

cells **A1** to **F17**.
Select the menu options **FORMAT-CELLS-BORDER** and, using Figure 2.3 as a guide, select **OUTLINE** and **THICK LINE** then **OK**. Remove the highlight from the cells and check that this border has been added.

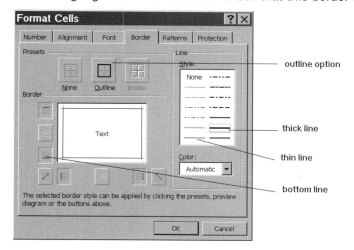

FIGURE 2.3

8. Use a similar technique to draw a thin line under cells **A8** to **F8**.

Note – **removing borders**. You can either use **EDIT-UNDO** to reverse changes or simply repeat the **FORMAT-CELLS - BORDER** command and click the **NONE** button.

9. **Independent Task.** Find the **BORDERS** button on the formatting Toolbar and use the down arrow next to it to:
Draw a line under row 16.
Give a right hand border to column A.

10. **Hiding Gridlines.** Now that we have borders we can dispense with gridlines; select the menu options **TOOLS-OPTIONS-VIEW** and then de-select the **GRIDLINES** option.

Note: When you come to print the worksheet you can still print the gridlines if you wish.

11. **Freezing Cells.** Once a worksheet gets larger it can be difficult to remember what the columns and rows represent once the labels have scrolled out of view.
To freeze them first select cell **B4** then take the menu options **WINDOW-FREEZE PANES.** Try scrolling and you will find that the cell labels remain 'frozen'.

Note: Use the **WINDOW-UNFREEZE PANES** command to reverse the process.

12. **Text Boxes.** Figure 2.4 shows a note added to the worksheet in the form of a text box. First make sure that the Drawing Toolbar is displayed (**VIEW-TOOLBARS**).
Click the **TEXT BOX** button then, starting near cell **C19**, draw the text box and type in the text shown.

Notes: Move or re-size a text box using the usual dragging techniques.

13

A selected text box can be deleted using the **DELETE** key, provided that the border is marked with dots, as shown in Figure 2.4, rather than diagonal lines.

	A	B	C	D	E	F
1		Finances - Spring Term				
2						
3	INCOME	Week 1	Week 2	Week 3	Week 4	Week 5
16						
17	Closing Balance	£ 840.00	£760.00	£680.00	£600.00	£520.00

FIGURE 2.4

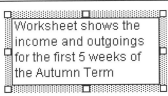

Worksheet shows the income and outgoings for the first 5 weeks of the Autumn Term

⑬ **Using Drawing Shapes.** You can add such shapes as arrows and circles to your worksheet, as shown in Figure 2.5. They are on the Drawing Toolbar. First encircle cell **F17**, using the **OVAL** button – the cell beneath may become invisible, if so then right click the oval and select the menu option **FORMAT AUTOSHAPE**. Select **NO FILL** from the **COLOR** drop-down box.
Next draw the arrow using the arrow button and finally create the text box. If you scroll down the worksheet the shapes move with the cells that they cover.

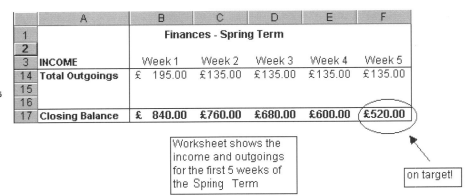

	A	B	C	D	E	F
1		Finances - Spring Term				
2						
3	INCOME	Week 1	Week 2	Week 3	Week 4	Week 5
14	Total Outgoings	£ 195.00	£135.00	£135.00	£135.00	£135.00
15						
16						
17	Closing Balance	£ 840.00	£760.00	£680.00	£600.00	£520.00

FIGURE 2.5

Worksheet shows the income and outgoings for the first 5 weeks of the Spring Term

on target!

⑭ **Viewing More Rows and Columns.** To view the maximum number of cells select the menu options **VIEW-FULL SCREEN**. You see more of the worksheet but important Excel components are hidden. Issue the command again to reverse it.
Another option is to use the **ZOOM** button on the standard toolbar to alter the scale of the worksheet. At the moment it probably displays 100%; try reducing it to, eg, 90%.

Printing a Worksheet

Printing in Excel is essentially the same as for other Microsoft and Windows based applications; you can specify which pages, number of copies etc are printed. We will briefly review them.

1   **Selecting Cells to Print.** Simply select the cells; however, once a worksheet gets over a certain length using the **SHIFT** key will simplify this, ie:

(a)   Select the top left of the cell range, eg cell A1.

(b)   Hold down the **SHIFT** key.

(c)   Scroll down to the bottom of the cell range.

(d)   Select the bottom right of the cell in the range.

2   **The Print Area.** The default area is the printed A4 page. To re-set it to a selected range of cells issue the menu commands **FILE-PRINT AREA-SET PRINT AREA**.

Now only the selected cells will be printed, not any blank ones outside the print area.

3   **Previewing the Printing.** Call up the print dialog box using **FILE-PRINT**. Select the **ACTIVE SHEETS** option in the **PRINT WHAT** section.

Click the **PREVIEW** button; the dialog box shows you how your printout will look on the page. Click the **SETUP** button now.

4   **Page Setup.** On the Page Setup dialog box select the **SHEET** tab. De-select the options **ROW AND COLUMN HEADINGS** and **GRIDLINES** if necessary; for a fairly small worksheet without too much detail it is usual to omit them.

Now select the **PAGE** tab and check the following settings.

(a)   **Orientation:** Portrait or Landscape.

(b)   **Paper size:**

(c)   **Fit to:** adjusts the print area to fit on one or more pages.

(d)   **Scaling:** adjusts the scale of the print area to fit the paper size.

5   **Margins and Alignment.** Select the **MARGINS** tab. Select the **HORIZONTALLY** and **VERTICALLY** options to centre the printed area on the page.

6   **Headers and Footers.** Select the **HEADER/FOOTER** tab.

First we will place your name and the date in the header and footer. Click **CUSTOM HEADER**. The dialog box is divided into three sections:

Place your name in the left-hand section then select the right hand section and click the **DATE** button to insert the current date.

Click **OK** and you are taken to the footer section; click on **NONE** and insert the page number. Close the Print dialog box now.

7   **Setting Page Breaks.** Open **VIEW** and select **PAGE BREAK PREVIEW**. You can use this window to reset the page breaks and the print area by dragging. You can also use it to cut and paste between different areas of the worksheet. Select **VIEW-NORMAL** to exit Page Break Preview.

15

(8) **Printing Out**. This is simply a matter of selecting **FILE-PRINT**.

Note: If your worksheet won't print check the correct printer is selected - check the Printer section of the Print dialog box. If the wrong area of the worksheet prints you can remove the print area and reset it – issue the menu commands **FILE-PRINT AREA-CLEAR PRINT AREA** and then reset it.

Consolidation - Check your Progress

(1) We will extend the Budget worksheet to cover 10 weeks. First select the column cells for week 5, **F3** to **F17,** and drag to select the next 5 columns G to K.

(2) Now use the **EDIT-FILL-RIGHT** to copy the data across – use **EDIT-UNDO** if you make a mistake.

(3) You will need to make some final adjustments:

(a) edit the week numbers for weeks 6–10

(b) delete the oval shapes which have also been copied

(c) amend the note in the text box

(d) delete or change unwanted cell borders.

Copying and Naming Worksheets

(1) We are going to copy the worksheet Sheet1 and then modify the copy. Click the **SHEET1** tab and then, holding down the **CTRL** key, start to drag it – the cursor is now marked with a '+' sign.

(2) Drag onto the Sheet2 tab and release the mouse button first followed by the **CTRL** key. Sheet1 is copied and renamed **Sheet1 (2).**

Note: If you forgot to hold down the **CTRL** key, or released it too soon, then you may have merely moved Sheet1 to a new position rather than copied it. In this case use the mouse to drag it back to its original position and try again.

(3) Click the tab for **SHEET1 (2)** if necessary. It opens, becoming the active worksheet; it is a replica of Sheet1. So we now have two identical worksheets with the default names **Sheet1** and **Sheet1 (2)**. We will rename them 'pessimistic forecast' and 'optimistic forecast'.

(4) Right click the **SHEET1** tab and select **RENAME**. The sheet tab is highlighted; type the new name 'pessimistic forecast'.

(5) Repeat this, renaming Sheet1 (2) 'optimistic forecast'. This time double click the sheet tab and then rename it.

Note: The longer the worksheet name the larger the tab, obscuring other sheet tabs. If this happens use the arrow buttons next to the sheet tabs to locate sheets.

Consolidation – Check your Progress

Copy the sheet 'optimistic forecast' again and rename it 'Spring Term'. Make the following changes to this sheet:

1 From week 4 onwards the cost of Accommodation rises to £70 a week.

2 Your parents send you £50 in week 8. Insert a row to hold this new category. Make sure that it is included in the formula to add the income rows.

3 You will be spending money on a concert in week 10. Modify the value in the 'Social' category for week 10 so that you end the Spring Term with £170.

Deleting a Worksheet from a Workbook

The workbook **Budget** now contains the 3 sheets – 'pessimistic forecast', 'optimistic forecast', and 'Spring Term'. We will delete 'pessimistic forecast'. Click the name tab for this worksheet and select **DELETE SHEET** from the **EDIT** menu.

Consolidation – Averages and Percentages

We will recap on some of the skills that we have learnt and also cover averages, percentages and absolute references. Create the worksheet shown in Figure 2.6 in a new workbook.

	A	B	C	D	E
1	Insurance Sales - Second Quarter				
2					
3		Home	Business	Holiday	Total Sales
4	April	587	148	89	
5	May	695	241	168	
6	June	734	198	207	
7					
8	Average Sales per Quarter				
9	Total Sales per Quarter				
10	% of Total				
11					

FIGURE 2.6

1 Format the new worksheet as shown above, ie title centred across columns A-E, cell labels in bold and values centred in cells. Save it as **Insurance Sales**.

2 We need to calculate the quarterly totals in cell **E4**. Use the **SUM** function to do this and then use the **EDIT-FILL-DOWN** command for cells **E5** and **E6**. Similarly calculate the totals in row 9 using **SUM** and **EDIT-FILL-RIGHT**.

17

3 To enter the average sales for each type of insurance in row 8 first select cell **B8** and enter the formula **=AVERAGE(B4:B6)**
Use **EDIT-FILL-RIGHT** to average the other insurance categories in cells C8 and D8.

4 Centre the values in the rows 8 and 9.
Use **FORMAT-CELLS-NUMBER** to remove any decimal places.

5 We can now express the quarterly totals held in cells B9 to D9 as fractions of the total sales – cell E9.
Enter the formula **=B9/$E$9** in cell **B10** (the '/' sign represents division, the dollar sign an absolute reference – see below).
The value 0.65732 is shown in cell B10 – this is the quarterly total for home insurance as a decimal fraction of the overall quarterly total.

6 *Note*: **Absolute and Relative References.** We have been using *relative* references in formulae so far; this is very useful as it means that whenever a cell containing a formula is copied or moved the formula is automatically adjusted. However, there are situations where we would not want this to happen; the percentages we are calculating are a case in point as they must all be based on cell E9. So we must have a way of making this clear, otherwise the formula would be adjusted when we used the Fill Right command. This is the reason for the dollar sign in the formula **=B9/$E$9** - E9 becomes an *absolute* reference while B9 remains a relative reference as we want it to change when it is copied to another cell. A quick way to convert a cell reference to an absolute one is to select the cell reference and press the F4 function key. Pressing it more than once gives a combination of relative and absolute references, called a *mixed* reference.

7 **Percentages.** Now to turn the B10 total into a percentage; open the **FORMAT** menu and select **CELLS** then **NUMBER**.
Select the **PERCENTAGE** option and make sure that **DECIMAL PLACES** are set to 2.
Home insurance is now shown as 65.73% of total sales.
Use **EDIT-FILL-RIGHT** to express Business and Holiday in cells C10 and D10 as percentages.

AutoFormat and Conditional Formatting

1 AutoFormat offers a range of pre-set formats; you can choose a complete worksheet or a range of cells and the various sections – headings, data, totals – will be correctly identified and formatted.
Select all the cells in the **Insurance Sales** worksheet. Open the **FORMAT** menu and select **AUTOFORMAT.** The dialog box shows a range of formats for you to review.
Select the **CLASSIC** 3 format and then **OK**.
Your worksheet is converted to the format chosen, but you may not be happy with its appearance, eg the columns may be too wide. To undo it issue the menu command **EDIT-UNDO AUTOFORMAT**.

② **Indenting, Rotating and Aligning Text**. Select cell range **A4** to **A10** in the **Insurance Sales** worksheet. Select the menu options **FORMAT-CELLS-ALIGNMENT**.

(a) **Indenting.** Increase the indent steps to 2 and click **OK**. Up to 15 indent steps are possible. Undo the indent.

(b) **Rotating Text.** Select the menu options **FORMAT-CELLS-ALIGNMENT** again and select 10 in the **DEGREES** box. Undo the rotation.

(c) **Aligning Text**. Use the dialog box again to centre the text horizontally and vertically.

③ **Conditional Formatting.** This can be used to emphasise those cells whose values meet certain limits.
Select cell range **B4** to **D6** and select the options **FORMAT-CONDITIONAL FORMATTING.**
Complete the dialog box to select cells whose values are between 100 and 200.
Now click the **FORMAT** button, then select the **BORDER** tab. Select the **OUTLINE** box.
Click **OK** on both dialog boxes; when you return to the worksheet you will see that the cell values meeting the conditions have a border.

④ **Copying Formats**. Using Format Painter you can copy complex formats quickly; first apply a range of formats to a cell, eg change the text in cell A4 to size 12, bold and colour it red.
Now identify the **FORMAT PAINTER** button, marked with a paintbrush on the Standard Toolbar. Simply click the button, click cell A4, then select a cell or a range of cells to copy the format to.

19

Excel Charts

Introduction

This topic provides an overview of Excel charts. Excel 2000 continues to use the ChartWizard to create charts from worksheet data, either embedded in the worksheet or in its own separate sheet. It also offers a full range of features to re-format the chart once it has been created.

Topic Objectives

- To practise the steps in ChartWizard.
- To create column, line and pie charts.
- To re-format and change the chart type.
- To chart non-adjacent cell ranges.
- To re-size charts to the size of the available window.

The Initial Worksheet Data

We will use the worksheet shown in Figure 3.1 as the basis for the charts in this topic; it analyses the number of holidays sold by country and time period. Create the column totals in row 12 using the **SUM** function and the **EDIT-FILL-RIGHT** command. Similarly create the totals in column F using **SUM** and **EDIT-FILL-DOWN**. The grand total in cell **F12** acts as a check that you have entered the holiday figures correctly.

Save the workbook as **Adventure Holidays**.

	A	B	C	D	E	F
1	Adventure Holidays					
2			Holidays Sold - India and Far East			
3						
4		1st Quarter	2nd Quarter	3rd Quarter	4th Quarter	Total
5						
6	China	80	93	188	96	457
7	Thailand	144	160	325	201	830
8	Tibet	72	66	90	64	292
9	Japan	120	90	288	88	586
10	India	120	146	350	223	839
11						
12	Total	536	555	1241	672	3004

FIGURE 3.

Using ChartWizard

Four ChartWizard dialog boxes guide you through the stages of chart creation:

1. Select the chart type – column, pie etc.

2. Select or change the range of cells that the chart is based on.

3. Select options for chart title, labels, axis etc.

4. Choose whether you want the chart to be on a separate sheet or part of the worksheet.

❶ **Column Charts.** Select the cell range **A6** to **B10** – the first quarter's sales. Issue the menu command **INSERT-CHART** (or use the ChartWizard button).

Note: The Office Assistant dialog box may appear too; you may find it useful as it supplements the standard ChartWizard instructions. It can be called up by clicking the **OFFICE ASSISTANT** button (marked with a '?') in the ChartWizard dialog box. It can be hidden by right clicking the Office Assistant logo and selecting **HIDE**.

❷ **ChartWizard – Step 1 of 4 – Chart Type** is displayed now. First select the **STANDARD TYPES** tab if necessary. The default chart type is **COLUMN** with 7 sub-types; as you select each sub-type Excel explains its purpose. Click the **PRESS AND HOLD TO VIEW SAMPLE** button – your chart is previewed. Finally select sub-type 1, the standard column chart and click the **NEXT** button.

ChartWizard – Step 2 of 4 – Chart Source Data. First select the **DATA RANGE** tab if necessary; you will see that the range of worksheet cells that you selected is confirmed – **A6** to **B10**. Excel shows them as absolute references. At this stage we could amend the range of cells we wanted to chart. Click the **NEXT** button.

ChartWizard – Step 3 of 4 – Chart Options. Using Figure 3.2 as a guide add titles and axis labels etc.

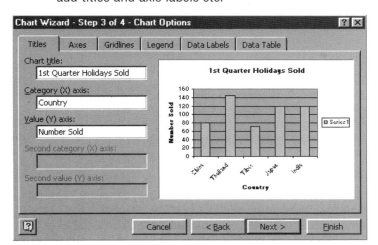

FIGURE 3.2

As this chart will not need a legend, click the **LEGEND** tab and de-select the option **SHOW LEGEND**.
Click the **NEXT** button.

ChartWizard – Step 4 of 4 – Chart Location. At this stage we can choose whether to have an 'embedded' chart – part of the worksheet – or place the chart in its own separate sheet.
Select **AS NEW SHEET** and click the **FINISH** button. The chart appears in its own sheet, with the default name **Chart1.**

Altering the Chart Size

You may find that when you first create a chart it is too small, and some of its elements are unreadable. You can alter its overall size with the View menu.

1 Make sure that the chart window is maximised then issue the menu command **VIEW-SIZED WITH WINDOW.** This command expands the chart to fill the window.
Next issue the menu command **VIEW-FULL SCREEN**; the chart is larger but you lose Excel menus and other features.

2 Issue the command **VIEW-FULL SCREEN** again to de-select this feature; click the **RESTORE** button and parts of the chart may be hidden by the reduced window size.

3 Now try the **VIEW-ZOOM** command which allows you to choose your own chart size.
Try out the **FIT SELECTION** option on the Zoom dialogue box – the chart fits to the current window size.

Note: The View-Zoom command is not available if Sized with Window is selected.

4 Finally open the **VIEW** menu and de-select the **FULL SCREEN** option and re-select **SIZED WITH WINDOW**.

5 *Note*: **The Chart Toolbar**. The Chart Toolbar sometimes appears when a chart is first created; close it for these activities as we will be using ChartWizard.

6 **Enlarging the Font Size.** To make the chart labels more readable right click the white space around the chart and select the option **FORMAT CHART AREA** and select the **FONT** tab. Change the font, eg to 8 point bold.

Changing the Chart Type

1 ChartWizard allows us to easily change one chart type to another. With **Chart1** as the active page in the workbook, select **CHART-CHART TYPE**.
Select **PIE** from the **STANDARD TYPES** tab. Keep sub-type 1.
When you click **OK** the column chart is re-plotted as a pie chart.

Adding a Legend. Pie charts show clearly the contribution of each value to the total, in this case the contribution of each holiday type to the total 'pie'. However, as a pie chart has no X or Y axis a legend is essential to explain the meaning of the the various pie sections.

Issue the menu command **CHART-CHART OPTIONS** and select the **LEGEND** tab.

Select the options **SHOW LEGEND** and **RIGHT** and click **OK**.

If the legend is too small it can be enlarged by dragging; the font size can be enlarged by right clicking the legend and taking the option **FORMAT LEGEND**.

Chart and Worksheet Windows

 It is often useful to see worksheet and related charts side by side rather than in separate windows – see Figure 3.3.

First check that the worksheet window is maximised and that the option **VIEW-SIZED WITH WINDOW** is selected.

Make sure **Chart1** is currently the active sheet. Issue the **WINDOW-NEW WINDOW** command.

Select the menu options **WINDOW-ARRANGE-VERTICAL**. Two identical chart windows appear; select the worksheet window containing the holiday data and your screen should resemble Figure 3.3.

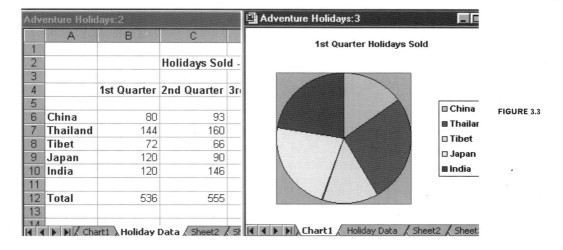

FIGURE 3.3

Chart and Worksheet Links

 A worksheet and the chart based on it are dynamically linked; when the data in one changes it also does in the other.

Make sure that the worksheet is the active sheet, select cell **B7** and change it to 500.

When the change is executed the section of the pie chart for Thailand changes too.

Issue the **EDIT-UNDO** command and the pie chart returns to its original form.

(2) Now select the Chart1 sheet if necessary and close it using the **CLOSE** button – the new window we opened is now closed. Maximise the remaining window.

Repositioning Pie Chart Segments

(1) We need to select the pie section for Tibet before we can move it; first click anywhere on the pie chart – not the grey surrounding area. Selection handles appear.

Now click once on the pie section for Tibet; handles appear on this segment.

(2) Now drag the segment slightly away from the main pie chart to emphasise it; press the **ESC** key to de-select the segment.

(3) *Note*: This sequence of selections can be fiddly at first; remember to use **EDIT-UNDO** if necessary. If you double click you will call up a dialog box which you can cancel.

Remember to check that the correct part of the chart is selected – enclosed in selection handles.

(4) Try out the following changes to your pie chart:

Drag the legend to enlarge it.

Click the grey area around the pie chart and drag to enlarge it.

Similarly try moving and re-sizing the title and inserting the word *Adventure* in the title.

Labelling Chart Values

(1) Pie charts often need the values of each segment shown if one is to make more than a rough guess at them. Select the menu options **CHART-CHART OPTIONS-DATA LABELS**.

(2) Try the various options in the dialog box – try each one, value, percent etc, finally choosing **SHOW PERCENT**.

(3) If the labels need enlarging then double click or right click on one of them. Select the **FONT** tab from the dialog box and select a different font size, bold etc.

Your pie chart should now look like Figure 3.4.

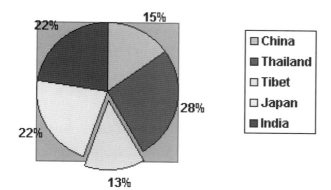

1st Quarter Adventure Holidays Sold

FIGURE 3.4

More Chart Formatting and Printing

1   **Text, Fonts and Style.** To format the pie chart title right click it and select **FORMAT CHART TITLE** then the **FONT** tab. Amend it, eg, to 12 Point Bold. Pressing the **ESC** key de-selects the title.

2   **Text and Arrows**. We will add a comment to the segment for Tibet; if the Drawing Toolbar is not displayed select **VIEW-TOOLBARS**.
Now use the same methods as you did for the workbook **Budget** in Topic 2 – see page 13 – to first draw the arrow. Use the text box button to add the comment *'What went wrong?'*. Re-format the text if necessary.

3   **Formatting All the Text in the Chart**. Click the extreme outside of the chart so that all of the chart – pie, label, legend etc – is selected. Then right click and take the option **FORMAT CHART AREA**. All the chart text will be affected by the changes.

4   **Printing**. This is the same in principle as printing a worksheet – see Topic 2, page 15. Select **FILE-PRINT** and make the usual checks using Print Preview and Page Setup.

25

Chart Colours and Patterns

1   If you decide to print in black and white you can add contrast to the segments, columns etc by the use of suitable patterns. Select a segment of the pie chart and select **FORMAT-SELECTED DATA POINT**.

2   Select the **PATTERNS** tab, and select suitable options from:
BORDER different edges.

     AREA   different patterns and colours – use the **FILL EFFECTS** button for monochrome patterns.

Line Charts

1 We will draw a line chart to compare holiday sales for Thailand and China for all 4 quarters. Select cells **A4** to **E7** of the worksheet.

2 Open the **INSERT** menu and select **CHART**.
The first ChartWizard dialog box is displayed. Select **LINE** and leave the default sub-type 4 selected. Click the **NEXT** button.

3 In the second ChartWizard dialog box check that the correct data range, ie **$A$4:$E$7** is displayed. Click the **NEXT** button.

4 Leave the 'Step 3 of 4' dialog box unchanged. Click the **NEXT** button.

5 In the fourth ChartWizard dialog box select **AS NEW SHEET**. Click the **FINISH** button.

6 The line chart, named **Chart2** appears. Select the options **VIEW-SIZED WITH WINDOW**. The line chart expands to fill the window – enlarge the window if necessary.

Adding Chart Legend and Title

1 The line chart lacks titles because we didn't add them in ChartWizard. Let's add them now. Take the options **CHART-CHART OPTIONS-TITLES**.

2 Enter **'Sales for China and Thailand'** in the **CHART TITLE** box.

3 Add the title **'Current Year'** to the **CATEGORY (X) AXIS** box.

4 In the **VALUE (Y) AXIS** box type the title **'Holidays Sold'**.

5 Now click the **LEGEND** tab and enable the **SHOW LEGEND** option.

6 Right click the chart and select **FORMAT CHART AREA** to enlarge the font.

Moving the Titles and Legend

1 Select the line chart and select the title for the Y axis, 'Holidays Sold'. Take the option **FORMAT-SELECTED AXIS TITLE-ALIGNMENT**.
Set the horizontal and vertical text alignment to **CENTER** and the **TEXT ORIENTATION** to 0 degrees if necessary. Click **OK**.

2 The Y axis label 'Holidays Sold' is now displayed horizontally; if it overlaps the chart you can drag it to move or re-size it. Use the **ENTER** key to divide the title into two lines.

3 **Independent Activities**.

(a) Use the option **FORMAT-SELECTED AXIS TITLE** to adjust the font size, style, colour etc of the X axis title, the X and Y axes themselves and the legend.

(b) Use the option **CHART-CHART TYPE** to change the line chart to another type of line chart returning to sub-type 4 when you have finished.

Drawing a Chart from Non-Adjacent Cells

1 If we wanted to draw a new chart comparing the holiday data for China and India we would need to select non-adjacent cell ranges from the worksheet, using the **CRTL** key.
First select the column headings **A4** to **E4** in the worksheet.

2 Hold down the **CTRL** key and select the 4 quarters for China – cells **A6** to **E6** – then the row for India – cells **A10** to **E10**.

3 You can now use ChartWizard to create a new line chart on a separate sheet – see Figure 3.5.
Add suitable titles and formatting. The chart should be named **Chart3**.

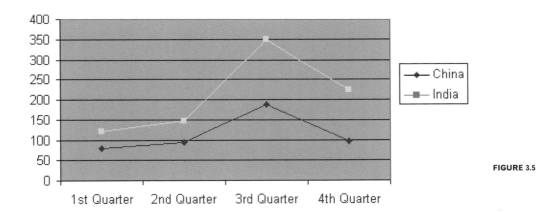

FIGURE 3.5

27

Naming and Copying Charts

The workbook **Adventure Holidays** contains one worksheet **Sheet1** and 3 charts named **Chart1**, **Chart2** and **Chart3**. If you have created other charts then these default numbers will be different.

We will give them more descriptive names. A chart name, like a sheet name, can be up to 31 characters long. It can contain spaces, but certain keyboard characters *cannot* be used, ie **[ ]**, /, \, **?** and *

1 Use the **FORMAT**-**SHEET**-**RENAME** command or double click on the sheet name tab to rename the sheets as follows:
Name the worksheet **Holiday Data.**
Name the pie chart **Pie1** and the line charts **Line1** and **Line2** respectively.

2 *Note*: **Copying and Deleting Charts**. Use the same drag and drop method that we used in Topic 2 to copy a worksheet – see page 16.

To delete a chart you can also use the same method as for a worksheet – select the name tab then use the **EDIT-DELETE SHEET** option. Check that you have selected the right sheet before confirming the deletion.

Remember that if you do delete the wrong sheet then closing the workbook without saving is a last resort although you will lose everything else since the last Save command!

Further Chart Operations

Introduction

This topic will cover some other types of chart plus using charts for goal seeking and for geographical data. It also reviews ways of plotting charts in three dimensions and reversing the chart axes.

Topic Objectives

- To add and remove values from a chart.
- To create area, embedded and 3-D column charts.
- To re-format and change 3-D charts.
- To change and reverse chart axes.
- To use the Excel Goal Seek feature in a chart.
- To add trendlines to a chart.
- To create a Chart Map of geographical data.

Changing the Scale of a Chart

1 Select the chart **Line2** in the workbook **Adventure Holidays.** You will see that the lines for India and China are quite close together but we can improve the chart's readability by changing the default scale for the vertical axis. At the moment the minimum and maximum values for the vertical axis are 0 and 400.

2 Right click the vertical axis and select the options **FORMAT AXIS** then **SCALE**.
Change the maximum and minimum values to 50 and 350. The chart values should be easier to compare. Review this by using the **EDIT-UNDO** and **RE-DO** commands.

Area Charts

Our next chart type is the area chart as shown in Figure 4.1. An area chart can be regarded as a number of line charts stacked on top of each other to form separate areas. It shows not just the trend in holidays sold for each country but the contribution of each country to overall sales.

1 Open the workbook **Adventure Holidays** if necessary. Select cells **A4** to **E10**, in the worksheet **Holiday Data**.

2 Create an area chart in ChartWizard, selecting sub-type 2.

3 At Step 3 of ChartWizard select the **DATA LABELS** tab then the **SHOW LABEL** option.

4 At Step 4 of ChartWizard select the **AS NEW SHEET** option.

5 Use the **VIEW-SIZED WITH WINDOW** command to re-size the window.

6 Add a chart title using the **CHART-CHART OPTIONS** command.

7 Format all the chart text to 9 point bold – right click the white space around the chart and select **FORMAT CHART AREA**.

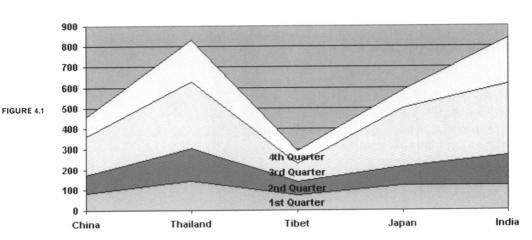

FIGURE 4.1

8 Name the chart **Area1**.

Removing and Adding Values to a Chart

1 In Excel it is straightforward to remove a range of chart values, eg a segment from a pie chart or an area from an area chart. It is equally easy to add a data range without needing to re-plot the whole chart.

2 **Removing Values.** Click once on the area for the 3rd quarter of the **Area1** chart (do not click on the area label). The area is enclosed in handles and the formula appears in the Formula Box with sheet name and absolute references added, eg =SERIES('Holiday Data'!$A$9,'Holiday Data'!$B$4:$E$5,'Holiday Data'!$B$9:$E$9,4).

3 Press the **DELETE** key to delete Quarter 3 (**EDIT-UNDO CLEAR** will reverse a mistake).

4 **Adding Chart Values.** Select the cell range **D4-D10** in the worksheet **Holiday Data**. This is the data range that we have just deleted. Copy it using **EDIT-COPY**.

30

⑤ Select the chart sheet **Area1** and use the **EDIT-PASTE** command. The 3rd quarter values are pasted back into the chart but are incorrectly positioned.

⑥ **Changing the Position of a Data Series.** Click the third quarter area of the chart again so that it is selected – enclosed in selection handles. Take the options **FORMAT-SELECTED DATA SERIES** then the **SERIES ORDER** tab.
Select the 3rd Quarter and move it to its correct position.

Reversing the Axes on a Chart

The **Area1** chart plots the countries along the X or horizontal axis – these are our 5 categories. The number of holidays sold per quarter is plotted on the Y or vertical axis. However, we could find it useful to reverse the axes, ie to have the quarters along the X axis and the number of holidays sold shown on the Y axis. Comparing Figures 4.1 and 4.2 will make this distinction clear. Because the chart is based on 4 quarters and 5 countries Excel will make the smaller number the values and the larger number the categories as this is more readable. However, it is easy to reverse this either in a new chart or for an existing one.

① With **Area1** the active sheet click the **CHARTWIZARD** button.
Check that Area Chart sub-type 2 is still selected. Click the **NEXT** button.

② **CHARTWIZARD-STEP** 2 is displayed next; make sure that the **DATA RANGE** tab is selected.

③ Click the **ROWS** button and the chart axes are reversed – you can preview this.
Click the **FINISH** button.

④ We now have 2 views of the same data:
Data Series in Columns – countries are categories, the quarters are plotted on the value axis – see Figure 4.1 above.
Data Series in Rows – the quarters are categories, the countries are plotted on the value axis – see Figure 4.2.
Note: You can reverse the axes for other chart types too.

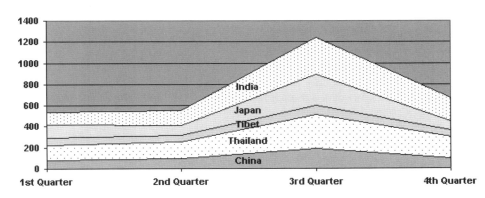

FIGURE 4.2

⑤ **Independent Activity**. Reverse the changes to the chart axes, showing the data series in columns again – see Figure 4.1 above.

Trendlines

1   Create the new workbook shown in Figure 4.3, naming it **Book Sales**.

FIGURE 4.3

	A	B	C	D	E
1			Book Sales		
2					
3	Month	No. Sold	Revenue	Advertising	
4	June	730	1990	180	
5	July	890	3030	305	
6	August	1055	3440	380	
7	September	1310	4421	640	
8	October	1600	5029	690	
9					
10					

2   Select cells **A3** to **D8** and create a standard column chart. Use the default settings for the chart axes, ie months as categories on the X axis.
Select the options **VIEW-SIZED WITH WINDOW** and format the text labels as before.

3   Click on one of the columns – all the columns in the same category should now be selected.
Take the options **CHART-ADD TRENDLINE-TYPE**.
Select **LINEAR** and then the **ADVERTISING** series; a trendline is added to the chart.
We can use trendlines to highlight trends or relationships between different sets of chart values, eg the sales and revenue for book sales continue to rise while advertising costs level off.

4   Name the sheet **Trend1**.

Goal Seeking

1   We have seen that worksheet and chart data are dynamically linked, ie changes in the worksheet are reflected in the chart. The reverse is equally true – amending chart values will change the worksheet.
Open the workbook **Adventure Holidays** and select the sheet **Holiday Data**.

2   Using the **CTRL** key select cell ranges **B4** to **F4** and **B12** to **F12**.
Create a standard column chart, accepting the default axis settings. Name the sheet **Goal Seek**.
Take the menu options **VIEW-SIZED WITH WINDOW**.

3   Execute the following steps:

(a) Click the 5th (total) column once.

(b) Click again – the column should now be selected.

(c) Place the pointer on the top of the column so that the pointer changes to a double-headed arrow. An information box will also open if the pointer is correctly positioned.

(d) Drag the column upwards until the value equals 3300. A Goal Seek dialog box appears – see Figure 4.4 – and the worksheet is displayed instead of the chart.

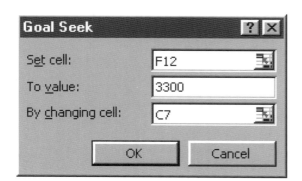

FIGURE 4.4

4 The idea now is to modify one of the cells in the range **B6** to **E10** to achieve the sales goal of 3300 holidays sold. Complete the 'By changing cell' box as shown in Figure 4.4.
The value of cell **C7** is changed to **456** – the number of holidays in Thailand you would need to sell to achieve the goal of 3300 in cell F12.

33

5 Click the **CANCEL** button on the dialog box to restore the cells to their previous values.

6 *Notes*: Goal seeking only works if the cell you change contains a value, not a formula. The cell whose value you set must also be related by a formula to the cell whose target value you are changing.
You can also goal seek in a worksheet – see page 72.

3-D Chart Concepts

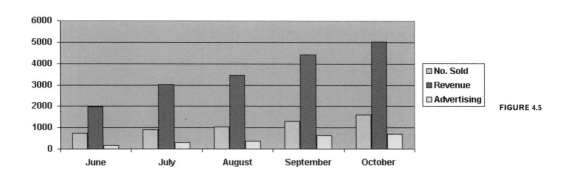

FIGURE 4.5

The column chart shown in Figure 4.5 displays 2 dimensions - the X axis showing the month categories and Y axis showing the data values.

The 3 dimensional chart shown in Figure 4.6 plots the same data in 3 dimensions, there is a third axis – the Z axis.

FIGURE 4.6

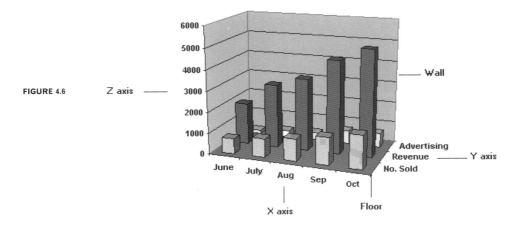

Briefly reviewing the different terminology for the 3-D chart:

The **X axis** remains the same – the category axis.

The **Y axis** becomes the new depth or inward axis now, plotting the three data series – No. Sold, Revenue, and Advertising.

The **Z axis** replaces Y as the value axis, showing the values for the three categories.

The 3-D chart has a base or floor and background walls.

Note: Excel offers 3-D versions of many of its chart types but not all of them offer a genuine third axis; some merely use three dimensions for visual effect.

Creating a 3-D Column Chart

1   Open the workbook **Book Sales** and make **Sheet1** the active sheet.

2   Select cells **A3** to **D8** and choose a column chart, sub-type 7 (3-D Column) in Excel. Name the chart sheet **3-D Column.**
Select the options **VIEW-SIZED WITH WINDOW** and format the text labels as before.
Your chart should now resemble Figure 4.6 above. Name it **3-D Column.**

3-D Chart – Formatting

1   **Changing Column Ordering.** We will bring the Advertising columns to the front so that they are not obscured by taller columns. Click one of the

Advertising columns and select the options **FORMAT-SELECTED DATA SERIES** then select the **SERIES ORDER** tab.
Select **ADVERTISING** in the **SERIES ORDER** box, then use the **MOVE UP** button to move Advertising to the front of the chart.

② **Chart Title**. Add a chart title using the options **CHART-CHART OPTIONS-TITLES**.
Add the title *'Book Sales Analysis'*.

③ *Note*: Use the same Insert and Format options as you would for 2-D charts. The ChartWizard button also offers the same options as before.

Selecting the Viewing Angle for a 3-D Chart

If you change the angle at which you view the 3-D data you can emphasise different elements of the chart. You can click and drag the elements directly or use a formatting menu which allows for more precise adjustment.

① With the chart **3-D Column** the active sheet take the options **CHART-3-D VIEW**.

② The dialog box appears shown in Figure 4.7; you may need to drag it to one side (use the Title Bar) to see the chart.

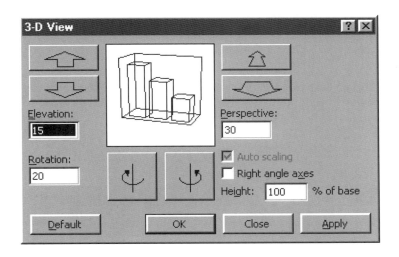

FIGURE 4.7

Try the following settings:

(a) Use the **UP** and **DOWN** arrow buttons above the **ELEVATION** box to vary the height at which you view the columns. Use the **APPLY** button to apply the new setting to the chart then the **DEFAULT** button to restore the standard setting.

(b) Use the **UP** and **DOWN** arrow buttons above the **PERSPECTIVE** box to vary the 3 dimensional depth or perspective. As before use the **APPLY** button to apply the new setting to the chart then the **DEFAULT** button to restore the standard setting.

(c)   Use the rotation arrow buttons next to the **ROTATION** box to rotate the chart about its vertical axis. As before use the **APPLY** button to apply the new setting to the chart then the **DEFAULT** button to restore the standard setting.

(d)   Amend the **HEIGHT % OF BASE** figure to 55 to alter the height of the chart relative to the base. As before use the **APPLY** button to apply the new setting to the chart then the **DEFAULT** button to restore the standard setting.
Close the dialog box.

Creating Embedded Charts

Instead of creating a chart in its own separate sheet we can embed it in the worksheet that it relates to. This is useful in saving space; it also allows you to view or print the chart and worksheet as one sheet.

1   Open the workbook **Insurance Sales** and select cell range **A3** to **D6**.

2   Create a standard bar chart. At ChartWizard Step 4 leave the option **AS OBJECT IN** selected and click **FINISH**.

3   *Notes*: Chart and worksheet can be selected in turn by clicking.
When one of the bars on the chart is selected Excel's Range Finder will highlight the associated cells in the worksheet.
The embedded chart can be moved or re-sized by dragging the selection handles.

4   **Drag and Drop** as a technique is used extensively in Excel; you can 'drag' a range of cells to select them and then 'drop' them onto a chart; this is particularly easy when the chart is embedded.
Select cell range **A8** to **D8** in the worksheet and locate the mouse pointer on the edge of this selected range as shown in Figure 4.8.

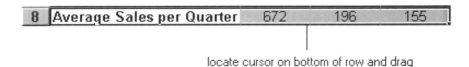

FIGURE 4.8

locate cursor on bottom of row and drag

Now simply drag the cell range (shown as a dotted rectangle) onto the chart – it now includes this fourth set of values.

5   *Notes*:

(a)   Use **EDIT-UNDO** to correct a mistake.

(b) Embedded charts can be formatted in the usual way - right click or double click the appropriate chart component.

(c) To place an embedded chart in a separate window temporarily first select it then take the options **VIEW-CHART WINDOW.**

(d) To transfer an embedded chart to its own separate sheet open ChartWizard and at Step 4 select **AS NEW SHEET.**

(e) Delete an embedded chart by selecting it and pressing the `DELETE` key.

Data Maps

If you have a worksheet containing geographical data (well-known place names, eg cities, countries) you can place the data on a map. Check first for the **DATA MAP** button on the Standard Toolbar – it is marked with a globe. If it is not installed then you will need the setup CD-ROM.

1   We will base the map on the new worksheet shown in Figure 4.9. Select all 10 cells.

County	No. of Staff
Lancashire	200
Cheshire	100
North Yorkshire	150
West Yorkshire	250

FIGURE 4.9

37

2   The data map will appear as an embedded chart. Click the **DATA MAP** button and drag to select a fairly large area close to the selected cells.

3   The toolbars change; if a dialog box appears, offering you a choice of maps, select **UK AND ROI COUNTRIES.**
The UK map may take some time to plot, especially if your data is on a diskette. Once drawn it can be 'dragged' to move or re-size it.

4   *Notes*: If a map control dialog box is shown close it for the moment.
If the Map Toolbar and the Map menus are not displayed `DOUBLE CLICK` on the map to select it.

5   **Re-sizing the Map.** The Map Toolbar has a drop-down box showing the scale – amend this to about 800%. Now use the hand-shaped **GRABBER** button to move the North of England into view, making sure that all 4 areas labelled in the worksheet – Lancashire, Cheshire, North and West Yorkshire – are visible.

6   **Adding Labels.** Click on the **MAP LABELS** button; a dialog box appears, select **MAP FEATURE NAMES.**
Move the screen pointer over the map until you find one of the 4 areas – Lancashire, Cheshire, North and West Yorkshire – then click it to add the

label.

To add the number of staff to the map click the **MAP LABELS** button again and select the **VALUES FROM-NO. OF STAFF** options.

Click each area again to label them with the numbers of staff.

7 Compare your map with Figure 4.10. Its exact appearance will be determined by the scale you have chosen and the exact part of the North of England that is in view.

The text labels can be formatted by right clicking them and selecting **FORMAT FONT**.

FIGURE 4.10

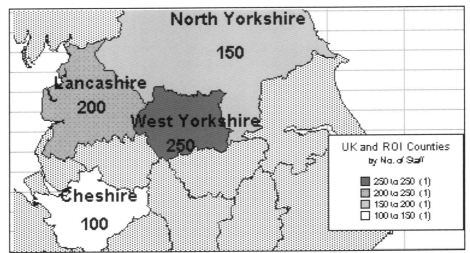

38

8 **Changing the Legend and Title**. Click the **SELECT OBJECTS** (arrow) tool on the Map Toolbar and double click the **LEGEND** box.

Make sure that the **LEGEND OPTIONS** tab is selected.

De-select the **USE COMPACT FORMAT** option if necessary.

Amend the title to **Northern Counties Staff**.

Independent Tasks

You may like to try out some other chart types that we have not covered; here are some ideas:

1 **Custom Charts**. Select the 10 cells shown in Figure 4.9. and start ChartWizard. At Step 1 click the **CUSTOM TYPES** tab and take time to preview the custom charts in the list. Some are highly formatted versions of standard chart types; others offer black and white formats – useful for monochrome printers. Other formats offer unusual ways of charting data that can sometimes be useful.

2 **Doughnut Charts.** A doughnut chart is similar to a pie chart but can show more than one data range. Construct one for the three months June to August (ie cell range A3 to D6) in the Book Sales workbook.

Excel Databases

Introduction

In Excel a database is really a type of list, a list being defined as a set of related data stored in the rows of a worksheet, eg a list of orders or invoices, details of club members or employees. Once organised in this way the list can be sorted or searched in various ways, ie it becomes a simple database.

Figure 5.1 shows an example of a simple list or database holding details of customer invoices. We can use it to introduce certain key database terms.

	A	B	C	D	E
1	Invoice Ref	Invoice Date	Customer No.	Customer Name	Invoice Value
2	A5418	08-Jun-00	2134	Singh Developments	658.00
3	A5419	05-Mar-00	1579	Berger Products	1437.00
4	A5420	31-Jan-00	2111	Webb Joinery	654.87
5	A5421	31-Jan-00	1093	Singh Electrical	2349.00
6	A5422	12-Apr-00	2198	Wilson's Golf	138.65
7	A5423	13-Apr-00	1532	Harris Publishing	2568.12
8	A5424	09-May-00	1579	Berger Products	188.00
9	A5425	09-May-00	2134	Singh Developments	19.91
10	A5426	20-Feb-00	1579	Berger Products	789.00
11	A5427	08-Mar-00	1478	Hamilton Media	905.99

FIGURE 5.1

Record. Each invoice occupies a row in the worksheet and is called a record.

Field. Each record holds the same 5 fields or data items – Invoice Ref, Invoice Date, Customer No, Customer Name and Invoice Value. Each field takes up a single column. The first row holds the field names, the other rows contain the actual data – the field values.

Database. The database consists of a list or table of 10 records.

Excel is primarily a spreadsheet application not a database and does not offer the relational, multi-table features of a special-purpose database management system such as Access. However, you can perform simple database-related tasks such as searching for individual records, adding and deleting records, editing existing records and sorting records into different sequences.

Topic Objectives

- To sort a list into various orders.
- To create new fields by calculation.
- To use a data form for database maintenance.
- To subtotal a database.
- To define search criteria using Excel's Advanced Filter.

▥ To search a database using logical operators.
▥ To extract records from a database.
▥ To use database statistical functions.
▥ To create PivotTables and PivotCharts.

Creating the Database

① **Inserting the Field Names**. Open a new workbook and enter the 5 field names shown in Figure 5.1 in cells **A1** to **E1**. Format as shown.

② **Using AutoComplete.** Complete columns C and D – the **Customer No**. and **Customer Name** fields – as shown in Figure 5.1 above. When you enter a customer name for the second time, eg Singh Developments, Excel completes the entry automatically. When this happens stop typing and continue with the next entry. You will need to be careful if there are two different companies starting with the same characters, eg 'Singh'; you would need to complete the rest of the company name.

Note: AutoComplete can be set on or off using the command **TOOLS-OPTIONS**.
Select the **EDIT** tab and choose **ENABLE AUTOCOMPLETE FOR CELL VALUES**.

③ Now complete column E, the **Invoice Value** field. Don't enter .00 after a value – see section 4 below.

④ **Decimal Formatting.** Format the **Invoice Value** fields to 2 decimal places, using the options **FORMAT-CELLS-NUMBER**.

⑤ **Data Series.** The **Invoice Ref** field is an alphanumeric sequence – increasing by 1 for every new invoice record. The Fill Series command is quicker to use when numbers, dates etc increase or decrease by a constant factor. For the fill operation to work they must be in adjacent cells.
Enter the start value A5418 in cell **A2**, then select the whole range, **A2** to **A11**.
Select the options **EDIT-FILL-SERIES**.
The dialog box shown in Figure 5.2 appears; make sure that the indicated options are selected (ie Series in: Columns, Type: Autofill, Step value: 1). The column is filled with a data series for the invoice references.
Note: A data series can also be based on weeks, dates and fractional numbers.

⑥ **Entering Dates**. You will find that you can enter dates in a number of formats and Excel will automatically recognise and format them.
Enter the first invoice date as *08jun* – Excel automatically converts it to 08-Jun; if it doesn't then check what you have entered.
Enter the remaining dates and check the status bar as you do so. Whatever the date format in the cells the status bar displays dates in a numeric format, eg 08/06/00.

⑦ Format all the dates to the one shown in Figure 5.1, using the options **FORMAT-CELLS-NUMBER-DATE**. Excel 2000 lets you use 4 digits for the year if you prefer.

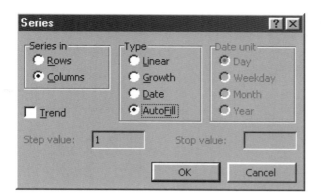

FIGURE 5.2

(8) Finally enter the rest of the data shown in Figure 5.1.

(9) Name the worksheet **Customer Invoices** and save the workbook as **Databases**.

Sorting Records

Often one needs to arrange the same list in different orders, eg in invoice number sequence (as at present) or in customer name sequence. Excel's Sort command can be used with any field or fields to place the records in a new sequence. This is useful in speeding up searching once the database gets larger.

Hints for Sorting

If there are different types of data in the fields that you are sorting then the sort order is as follows: Numbers, text, logical values, error values, blanks.

Use the **EDIT-UNDO SORT** command to reverse an incorrect sort.

Remember to include all the rows and columns in the sort, ie all fields, all records. If you leave any columns out they will become attached to the wrong record.

(1) To sort the customer invoices into date sequence select the whole database, ie cells **A1** to **E11** including the field names in the header row. Take the menu options **DATA-SORT**.

(2) Complete the Sort dialog box as shown in Figure 5.3:
SORT BY: We will sort by **Invoice Date**; select this field from the **SORT BY** box.
Leave **ASCENDING** selected (ie earliest dates first).
THEN BY: We are only sorting by one field so leave these 2 options unselected.
MY LIST HAS: HEADER ROW should remain selected – we do not want the field names in row 1 to be sorted, only the records. Click **OK**.
The records in the database are sorted into date order, earliest dates first.
Note: If you have made a mistake use **EDIT-UNDO SORT**.

(3) **Sorting by More than One Field.** If we sort the records in date order by customer we use two fields or 'keys' in database parlance. The primary key

FIGURE 5.3

is the customer name and the invoice date the secondary key.
Select all the database cells as before and issue the **DATA-SORT** command.
Make the following entries in the Sort dialog box:

(a)   In the first **SORT BY:** box select **Customer Name**.

(b)   In the first **THEN BY:** dialog box select **Invoice Date**.

(c)   Select the **DESCENDING** button next to the first **THEN BY**: box; this will place them in reverse date order, ie latest invoices displayed first.

(d)   Click **OK** and check that the records are sorted into this new sequence.

4   **Consolidation.** Try the following sorts:

(a)   Invoices in descending order of value, ie largest value invoices first.

(b)   By **Customer Ref** in ascending date order.

Calculated Fields

We will add two new database fields:

a.   A field calculating VAT at 17.5%.

b.   A **Total** field which adds the VAT field to the **Invoice Value** field.

Both fields are calculated fields, ie produced by formulae.

1   Enter the field names **VAT** and **Total**, in cells **F1** and **G1** – see Figure 5.4.

2   In cell **F2** enter a formula that calculates 17.5%, ie =**E2*0.175**.
Copy the formula to the rest of the records using the **EDIT-FILL-DOWN** command.

3   Now enter a formula in cell **G2** to add the **VAT** field to the **Value** field and fill down as before.

4   Format the two new fields to 2 decimal places.

5 Now sort the database by the **Total** field – you will find that calculated fields can be sorted like the other fields. Compare the database with Figure 5.4.

	A	B	C	D	E	F	G
1	Invoice Ref	Invoice Date	Customer No.	Customer Name	Invoice Value	VAT	Total
2	A5425	09-May-00	2134	Singh Developments	19.91	3.48	23.39
3	A5422	12-Apr-00	2198	Wilson's Golf	138.65	24.26	162.91
4	A5424	09-May-00	1579	Berger Products	188.00	32.90	220.90
5	A5420	31-Jan-00	2111	Webb Joinery	654.87	114.60	769.47
6	A5418	08-Jun-00	2134	Singh Developments	658.00	115.15	773.15
7	A5426	20-Feb-00	1579	Berger Products	789.00	138.08	927.08
8	A5427	08-Mar-00	1478	Hamilton Media	905.99	158.55	1064.54
9	A5419	05-Mar-00	1579	Berger Products	1437.00	251.48	1688.48
10	A5421	31-Jan-00	1093	Singh Electrical	2349.00	411.08	2760.08
11	A5423	13-Apr-00	1532	Harris Publishing	2568.12	449.42	3017.54
12							

FIGURE 5.4

Using a Data Form

We will briefly review using a data form to search a database; it is limited to displaying one record at a time. We cover more advanced search methods later in this topic.

1 Select one of the cells in the Customer Invoices database – there is no need to select the whole database.

2 Select the options **DATA-FORM**. The data form shows the field names and the first record on the left. It also shows the number for the current record eg 1 of 10.

3 We can enter various search criteria to locate records:

(a) Click the **CRITERIA** button on the data form – the blank record allows you to enter search criteria.
Enter ***Singh*** in the **Customer Name** field in either upper or lower case.

(b) Click the **FIND NEXT** button and the first record that meets this search criterion is displayed; click **FIND NEXT** again to find any further matching records. There are 3 records in all. Click the **FIND PREV.** button to scroll back again.

Note: Both company names beginning in 'Singh' are located – to narrow the search further we would have to enter the complete company name.

(c) Click the **CRITERIA** button. 'Singh' is still displayed in the **Customer Name** field.
Enter the second criterion **<1000** in the **Invoice Value** field.
We will search using 2 criteria, ie customer name = Singh *and* invoice value less than £1000.
Click the **FIND NEXT** button. Two records match these criteria.

(d) Click **CRITERIA** then the **CLEAR** button to delete the search criteria, then click the **FORM** button to display the data form.

4 **Editing Records.** First use the data form to locate the record for invoice

number A5422. Amend the Customer Ref to 2199.
Close the data form.

Notes: The two calculated fields, **VAT** and **Total**, cannot be edited in the data form as they are based on formulae which should not be overwritten. Care needs to be used when editing records in a data form as amendments are saved *permanently* as soon as you move to another record. Make sure that you use the **RESTORE** button *before* you move to another record.

Subtotalling a Database

Excel has a special subtotal command for databases; this is not only quicker than using the SUM function but includes other useful outlining features, as we will see.

1 Select all the cells in the **Customer Invoices** database and sort it in **Customer Name** order – we will subtotal the invoices for each customer.

2 Issue the **DATA-SUBTOTALS** command. Complete the dialog box as follows, using Figure 5.5 as a guide.

(a) **AT EACH CHANGE IN**: Select **Customer Name**.

(b) **USE FUNCTION**: Leave this as **SUM** as we are adding the value of invoice values.

(c) **ADD SUBTOTAL TO**: Select **Total** – the field values we are adding.

(d) Click **OK**.

FIGURE 5.5

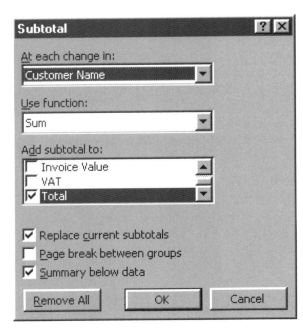

③ You will see that after each customer a new row holds the customer name and a subtotal for the value of their invoices. A grand total for all invoices is displayed at the end of the database.

④ **Outlining a Database**. Three buttons, labelled 1, 2 and 3, are displayed at the top left of the screen. They provide different outlines – click each in turn:
BUTTON 2 – the records are hidden and only the subtotals and grand total are displayed.
BUTTON 1 – only the grand total is displayed.
BUTTON 3 – the records, subtotals and grand totals are all displayed again.

⑤ Experiment with the **MINUS** buttons on the left of the screen – you can hide individual groups of records so that only the subtotals are displayed. The button then changes to a '+' sign. Click it again to re-display them.

⑥ **Removing Subtotals**. Issue the command **DATA-SUBTOTALS** then click the **REMOVE ALL** button in the dialog box. The database is now displayed without subtotals.

Searching Using Advanced Filter

Using the Excel Advanced Filter option you can search on more than two fields, and use a wider range of operators than a data form.

① We will use a new database for these searches; it contains details of domestic helpers who work as cleaners, babysitters etc in various areas – see Figure 5.6.

	A	B	C	D	E	F
1	Surname	First Name	Area	Skill	Age	Available
2	Duncombe	Emma	Moordown	Ironing	38	11-May
3	Green	Barry	Kinson	Cleaning	62	12-May
4	Bray	Ian	Upton	Babysitting	37	19-May
5	Hamilton	Ann	Moordown	Ironing	41	22-May
6	Crabb	Denys	Christchurch	Cooking	53	21-May
7	Harding	Chris	Christchurch	Painting	56	25-May
8	Wingfield	Helen	Upminster	Babysitting	31	29-May
9	Moore	Ian	Kinson	Washing up	48	29-May
10	Webb	Wayne	Whitchurch	Painting	18	29-May
11	Turner	Maria	Christchurch	Washing up	43	01-Jun
12	Cox	Tracey	Kinson	Babysitting	30	01-Jun
13	Holding	Ted	Parkstone	Cleaning	22	03-Jun
14	Turner	Vivien	Purewell	Ironing	39	29-Jun
15	Foster	John	Moordown	Cooking	67	04-Jun

FIGURE 5.6

Open a new workbook and save it as **Domestic Help**. Create and format the worksheet as shown.

Note: Make sure that the details are exactly as shown, otherwise the searches that follow may not work.

② **Defining a Database.** First we need to define this range of cells as a database.

Select **A1** to **F15** – all the cells in the database; these are the 14 records plus the headings in row 1.
Select the **INSERT** - **NAME** - **DEFINE** options.
Enter the name **Database** in the dialog box and click the **OK** button. You have now defined the database and the headings are identified as field names.

3   **Defining the Search Criteria.** Use the Edit menu to copy cell range **A1** to **F1**, ie all 6 field names.
Paste them into row 17, starting at cell **A17**.

4   **Notes on search criteria**:

(a) These cells are your **criteria range** – the fields you are using to search.

(b) You don't need to include all the field names, only those that you need for your search.

(c) Place the criteria range at any suitable point on the worksheet – they are best near the database you are searching.

5   **Entering Search Criteria.** The first row of cells (row 17) contains the names of the fields you can search; you merely enter your search criteria in the next row of cells, row 18.
Let's locate all the records for the skill 'ironing' first.
Enter **Ironing** in cell **D18** beneath the field name **Skill** – see Figure 5.7 (upper or lower case is OK, the search is not case sensitive).
Press **ENTER** or click the tick box now or the next stage will not work.

	A	B	C	D	E	F
17	Surname	First Name	Area	Skill	Age	Available
18				ironing		
19						

FIGURE 5.7

6   **Advanced Filter.** Select the menu options **DATA-FILTER-ADVANCED FILTER**.
Complete the Advanced Filter dialog box, using Figure 5.8 and these instructions as a guide:

(a) **Action: Filter the List, in place.** Leave this selected; Excel will filter out records not matching the search criterion 'Ironing'.

(b) **List Range**: You need to specify the list or database you are searching. Check the cell references – see Figure 5.8 below – and modify them if not correct.

(c) **Criteria Range**: Check that the cell range holding your search criteria (see sections 3 and 4 above) are the same as in Figure 5.8 below.

(d) Check no other options are selected and click **OK**. The 3 records for ironing are selected. If not try again, checking the cell references very carefully.

7   Select the menu options **DATA-FILTER-SHOW ALL**. This ends the search and re-displays the database.

8   Add a further search criterion, 'Moordown' in cell **C18**.
Use the **ADVANCED FILTER** option again; you will find that only two records now match the second criterion; the other record is filtered out.
Select the menu options **DATA-FILTER-SHOW ALL**.

46

FIGURE 5.8

9   **Comparison Operators.** You can use the following 6 operators to narrow down your searches:

=	equal to (not needed on its own)
<	less than
>	greater than
<>	not equal to
<=	less than or equal to
>=	greater than or equal to

10   Use these operators in the following three searches:
All helpers living in Christchurch (no operator needed).
All helpers aged 53 or over.
Kinson helpers available after 28 May (enter a valid date first *then* the > operator).

11   **Hints for Advanced Filter.** Remember to erase previous search conditions where necessary, otherwise you will filter out the wrong records.
If you forget to press ENTER after entering the search criterion the menu commands will be unavailable.
Use the **DATA-FILTER-SHOW ALL** to re-display all the records before starting the next search.
If no records are selected check that the search criteria are correct and entered under the correct field name. Also check that the cell coordinates in the Advanced Filter dialog box are correct, see Figure 5.8 above.

12   **'Wildcards'.** The * and ? characters can be used as 'wild cards', ie to represent one or more characters. Try using them in the following three searches:

(a) Enter ***church*** in cell **C18** as your search condition. Records for both Christchurch and Whitchurch are located, as the * symbol can substitute for any combination of adjacent characters.

(b) If we are unsure if the forename 'Denys' is spelled with a 'y' or an 'i', the '?' character can be used to substitute for a single character.
Enter ***Den?s*** under the first name field and the record for Denys Crabb will be located.

(c) Enter **Up** under the **Area** field. Records for both Upminster and Upton are located, ie if you can supply the starting characters of the search criterion you don't need a wildcard character.
Restore all 15 records and remove any search criteria from row 18.

13 **Using 'And' and 'Or'.** So far we have implicitly been using 'AND' to combine two search conditions; ie for a record to be selected both conditions needed to be met, eg Poole area AND available 25 July.
However, the 'OR' condition is equally useful, eg Poole or Purewell area, age under 30 or over 50.
Let's retrieve records for areas Parkstone or Purewell; this involves entering the 2 criteria in 2 different rows.
Enter **Parkstone** in the first cell below the **AREA** criterion – cell **C18.**
Enter **Purewell** in the second cell below the **AREA** criterion – cell **C19.**

14 We will need to amend the criteria range as they occupy 2 rows.
Use the **DATA-FILTER-ADVANCED FILTER** command and select the **CRITERIA RANGE:** box.
Amend it to the references shown in Figure 5.9.

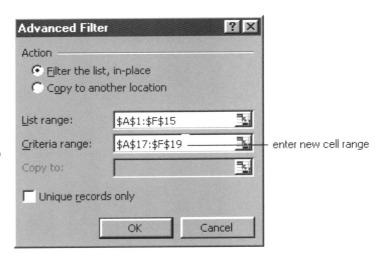

FIGURE 5.9

Click **OK** and the 2 records matching either search condition are selected.
Restore all 15 records as before.

15 We can also combine 'AND' and 'OR', eg Ironing for Moordown or Cooking for Christchurch.
The logic is (Ironing AND Moordown) OR (Cooking AND Christchurch).
Enter the search criteria as shown in Figure 5.10.

	Surname	First Name	Area	Skill	Age	Available
17						
18			moordown	ironing		
19			christchurch	cooking		
20						

FIGURE 5.10

Run **ADVANCED FILTER** – 3 records are selected, matching both pairs of criteria.

(16)   **Independent Activities.** Carry out the following searches:

(a) All helpers over 59 or under 20.

(b) Any cook available before 20 May or after 2 June (you will have to enter the job criterion twice – on both rows).

(c) Excel also offers an AutoFilter database search feature; it is fairly self-explanatory; select **DATA-FILTER-AUTOFILTER** then use AutoFilter to select helpers living in Christchurch or Upton. Select **DATA-FILTER-AUTOFILTER** again to turn off this feature.

Extracting Database Records

In a real-life situation a database could become too long to use conveniently; a solution is extract a subset of the records from the main database to use separately. We can do this using Excel's Advanced Filter in a very similar way to the method used for searching.

(1)   **Database Definition.** Open the workbook **Databases** and then the worksheet **Customer Invoices**. Select all the records in the database, including the row holding the field names.
Select the menu options **INSERT-NAME-DEFINE**.
Enter the name *Database* in the Name dialog box and click **OK**; this defines the cells as a database.

Note: It is a good idea to re-define the database every time it is opened for use – if records have been added or deleted this will change the number of rows etc. in the database.

(2)   **Copying the Search Criteria**. Select all the field names in row 1 and issue the **EDIT-COPY** COMMAND.
Paste them in row 13, starting at cell **A13**.

(3)   **Enter the Extract Criteria.** To extract all invoice records totalling less than £1000 enter the criterion <1000 in cell **G14**.

(4)   **Choosing the Extract Range.** Take the options **DATA-FILTER-ADVANCED FILTER**. When the Advanced Filter dialog box opens do the following:

(a) Select **COPY TO ANOTHER LOCATION**.

(b) Check that the cell references in the **LIST RANGE**: box match the cell references in your database range – see Figure 5.11. If not change them.

(c) Select the **CRITERIA RANGE**: box and check the cell references match those shown in Figure 5.11. These are the cells where we enter the search criteria.

(d) Select the **COPY TO**: box and check the cell references match those shown in Figure 5.11. These are the cells where the extracted records will be copied to.

(e) **Note**: A quicker way of checking or amending the cell ranges is to click the Collapse Dialog button next to the appropriate box – see Figure 5.11. This shrinks the dialog box and you can select the cell range by 'dragging' rather than have to type it in. To restore the size click the Collapse Button again.

FIGURE 5.11

⑤ Check that records matching the search criterion (Total < 1000) have been extracted to row 17 below the field headings.

⑥ **Note**:. Any records already in the extract range will be overwritten by the extracted data and permanently lost; you cannot undo an extract operation (unless you exit the worksheet without saving it). This means that you must be careful to place the extracted records where this cannot happen; another option is to place a limit on the number of rows you extract when you define it at the risk of not extracting every relevant record.

⑦ **Independent Task.** First clear the search condition from cell **G14** and the extracted records from row 17 and below.
Extract all the records where the invoice date is on or before 08-Mar. Use the full date format in your search, eg 08/03/00. 5 records should be extracted.

Note: Remember to select **COPY TO ANOTHER LOCATION** again – see section 4a above – the cell range should remain the same.

Database Functions

Excel provides special database functions, eg DSUM, DAVERAGE, DMIN, DMAX, to filter out certain database records and analyse them. Unlike the ordinary statistical functions such as SUM and AVERAGE you can combine them with search criteria, eg the average invoice value for a particular customer.
Database functions are composed of 3 elements, eg for the function DSUM it is **DSUM(database,"field",criteria)**:

◻ **database** is the name of the cell range that you have defined as a database – see previous task
◻ **field** is the name of the field that you wish to add up or sum
◻ **criteria** is the criteria range that you have defined using Advanced Filter – see previous task.

You can type in these three elements, but it is preferable to follow the steps in Paste

Function, especially if you only use them infrequently.

1 Make sure that the workbook **Databases** and the worksheet **Customer Invoices** is open. Check the following database and criteria ranges still apply:
Select **INSERT-NAME-DEFINE**. Select the name **DATABASE** and check it still refers to cells **$A$1:$G$11**.
Select the name **CRITERIA** and check it still refers to cells **$A$13:$G$14**. If necessary reset them.

Note: The Name Box on the left of the Formula Bar also allows you to review the names used in a workbook. A name once defined is available to any sheet in the workbook.

2 Now remove any extract range remaining from the previous task from row 17 downwards.

3 We will place several database functions below the database. Enter the titles shown in Figure 5.12, starting in cell **A16**.

	A	B	C	D	E	F	G
13	Invoice Ref	Invoice Date	Customer No.	Customer Name	Invoice Value	VAT	Total
14							
15							
16	No of Invoices	Ave. Value	Total Value	Total VAT	Min Value		
17							
18							

FIGURE 5.12

4 **Paste Function.** First we will use the DSUM function to total up the VAT that *Berger Products* have to pay on their invoices.
Enter *Berger Products* in cell **D14** – this is our search term.
Now select cell **D17** - this is where the database function will be entered.
Click the **PASTE FUNCTION** button – on the Standard toolbar and marked *fx*.

51

5 When the Paste Function dialog box appears select **DATABASE** from the **FUNCTION CATEGORY** list.
Select **DSUM** from the **FUNCTION NAME** list and click **OK**.
If the Office Assistant opens close it for now.

6 A dialog box appears. Complete the next dialog box as follows:
Enter *Database* in the **DATABASE** box – the name of the database defined in the previous task.
Enter *"VAT"* in the **FIELD** box (in double quotes) – the field to be summed.
Enter *Criteria* in the **CRITERIA** box – the name of the criteria range.

7 If you have completed Paste Function correctly the total VAT paid on Berger Products invoices is placed in cell **D17**. The formula **=DSUM(database,"VAT",criteria)** displays in the Formula Bar.

Note: If you get an error message then check:
- each name is spelt correctly
- the field name is entered in double quotes
- there are no spaces in the formula
- you have placed the = sign, commas and brackets correctly.

You can edit the formula in the Formula Bar – formulae are not case sensitive.

8 Click the **PASTE FUNCTION** button again and use **DSUM** again to calculate the total value of invoices for Berger Products in cell **C17**.

9 We will enter a formula directly; this time to count the number of invoices for Berger Products.
Select cell **A17** then enter the formula =**DCOUNT(database,"total",criteria)**

10 Select cell **B17** next and calculate the average value of an invoice for Berger Products. The formula is =**DAVERAGE(database,"invoice value",criteria)**

11 **The Office Assistant.** The DMIN function is used to find the lowest value in a range of database cells. We will use Office Assistant to locate this function and then find the invoice with the lowest total value.
Select cell **E17** and select Paste Function. If the Office Assistant dialog box is not displayed click the Office Assistant button, marked with a '?', at the bottom left of the Paste Function Dialog box and select 'Help with this feature' (if nothing happens then Office Assistant has not been installed).

12 Enter a brief description of the function you want in the next dialog box, eg *find the minimum value in a database* and click **SEARCH**. Office Assistant should select one or two functions based on your description.

Note: This feature is useful if you don't know the name of the function but can describe it. However, it depends heavily on your using the appropriate search terms and narrowing down the search to the function(s) that you want. So if you used the word 'lowest' instead of 'minimum' in your description Office Assistant may not find the function. If you prefer you can use Keywords, eg, 'database' and 'minimum'.

13 Select **DMIN** from the list and exit Office Assistant.
Now complete the Paste Function dialog box. The formula in cell **E17** should read =**DMIN(database,"total",criteria)**.

14 Format cells **B17** to **E17** to 2 decimal places. Now compare the values with Figure 5.13.

FIGURE 5.13

	A	B	C	D	E	F	G
12							
13	Invoice Ref	Invoice Date	Customer No.	Customer Name	Invoice Value	VAT	Total
14				Berger Products			
15							
16	No of Invoices	Ave. Value	Total Value	Total VAT	Min.Total		
17	3	804.67	2836.45	422.45	220.90		

15 Once we have entered database function formulae we can use different search conditions, eg customer reference.
Clear the search condition 'Berger Products' from cell **D14**.
Enter 2134 in cell **C14**; every time the search criteria in row 14 are changed the formulae immediately recalculate the new results.

16 **Consolidation – Search Criteria.** Enter the following search criteria, remembering to clear previous ones before you enter the next:

(a) Invoice numbers A5420 onwards.

(b) Invoices with VAT amounts less than £150.

(c) Invoices totalling less than £700 or more than £2000 (you will need to reset the criteria range to use an 'OR' condition – see previous task).

PivotTables

Using a PivotTable you can rearrange the columns and rows of a database to present the data in new ways. Often it is quicker and easier than using formulae or queries and can be used to produce a formatted report.

1 Make sure that the workbook **Databases** and the worksheet **Customer Invoices** is open.

2 We will create a PivotTable that shows the total invoices placed by each customer over time. Figure 5.15 shows part of the completed table.

3 Take the options **DATA-PIVOTTABLE** and **PIVOTCHART REPORT**. On Step 1 of the PivotTable Wizard accept the defaults 'Microsoft Excel List or Database' and 'PivotTable' and click **NEXT**.

4 Step 2 of the PivotTable Wizard confirms that the range of cells named 'database' will be used. Click **NEXT**.

5 On Step 3 of the PivotTable Wizard click **NEW WORKSHEET** then **LAYOUT**.
The PivotTable outline is displayed, letting you drag the various fields onto the outline in order to design your PivotTable. Do the following using Figure 5.14 as a guide:

(a) Identify the **CUSTOMER NAME** field button; it will be our first row on the PivotTable. Drag and drop it on the section of the PivotTable outline labelled 'Row'.

(b) Identify the **INVOICE DATE** button; it will be our first column on the PivotTable. Drag and drop it on the section of the PivotTable outline labelled 'Column'.

(c) The PivotTable will summarise the **invoice value**, **total** and **VAT** for each customer. Drag and drop these 3 items on the section of the PivotTable outline labelled 'Data'.
Click the **OK** button then the **FINISH** button.

6 The PivotTable is created in its own worksheet; name it **PivotTable1**. It should resemble Figure 5.15 (first part only shown). If not then:

(a) Make the table more readable – reformat the numeric data in columns C to K to 2 decimal places and widen column A if necessary.

(b) You may get the error message 'Enable Selection button on Select submenu..... is not pressed in'. If so then de-select the cells and right click the worksheet. A menu appears. Choose **SELECT-ENABLE SELECTION** and try again.

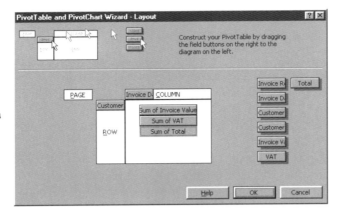

FIGURE 5.14

FIGURE 5.15

	A	B	C	D
3			Invoice Date ▼	
4	Customer Name ▼	Data ▼	31-Jan-00	20-Feb-00
5	Berger Products	Sum of Invoice Value		789
6		Sum of VAT		138.075
7		Sum of Total		927.075
8	Hamilton Media	Sum of Invoice Value		
9		Sum of VAT		
10		Sum of Total		

7   **Re-Organising the PivotTable**. You can re-organise your PivotTable indefinitely to give you different views. Dragging the labels/buttons 'Customer Name', 'Data' and 'Invoice Date' changes their order in the table.

Try this as follows, remembering you can reverse an action using **EDIT-UNDO**.

(a) Drag the **CUSTOMER NAME** button to the other side of the **DATA** button – the table is re-ordered.

(b) Drag the **CUSTOMER NAME** button to the right of the **INVOICE DATE** button.

(c) The down arrows on the field buttons allow you to hide certain records from the PivotTable – try this.

(d) You can improve the appearance of the PivotTable with a range of AutoFormats, accessed from the Format menu. Experiment with these. If you wish you can also use indenting and conditional formatting.

8   *Note*: PivotTables support many of the operations of standard worksheets, eg formatting, sorting, merging cell labels and calculated fields. The special PivotTable Toolbar offers other features too.

Creating a PivotChart

Once you have created a PivotTable you can create a PivotChart based on it, provided that both are in the same workbook. The normal relationship between chart and associated data applies, ie when one changes so does the other; their exact relationship is explained in the Excel Help text.

1 Make sure that **PivotTable1** is the active sheet.
First make sure that a cell outside the PivotTable is selected then click the **CHARTWIZARD** button (or use the **INSERT-CHART** option).

2 **CHARTWIZARD STEP** 1 appears; select a pie chart and click the **NEXT** button.

3 **CHARTWIZARD STEP** 2 appears; select the **DATA RANGE** tab if necessary. Click the **DATA RANGE** box then click one of the cells in PivotTable1 and the cell references in the **DATA RANGE** box will now include the whole PivotTable. Click the **NEXT** button.

4 **CHARTWIZARD STEP** 3 appears. Make your selections of titles, legend and data labels and click the **NEXT** button.

5 **CHARTWIZARD STEP** 4 appears. Place the chart as a new sheet then press the **FINISH** button.

6 Open the **VIEW** menu and select the option **SIZED WITH WINDOW**. The PivotChart expands to fill the window space available.

7 Right click the blank area around the pie and select the option **FORMAT CHART AREA**.
Enlarge the font to, eg, size 9, bold.

8 Now experiment with the three drop down boxes for customer name, data and invoice date. You can use them to remove various sets of values. If you check the PivotTable1 sheet after doing this you see that the values have been removed from the PivotTable too.

Using Linked Workbooks

Introduction

If you link workbooks together they can share common data. Although you could link worksheets within a single workbook, sometimes separate but linked workbooks are more convenient, eg if several workbooks are created separately and then combined later. As linked workbooks are linked by formula then changes made to one workbook will automatically update the others. Linked workbooks can also be opened and closed as a group. We will use as our example the branches of a car hire company where the same financial data is recorded for each branch, and then summarised.

Topic Objectives

- To create an Excel template.
- To locate workbooks using Excel's search features.
- To link workbooks with external formulae and Paste Link.
- To save related workbooks as a workspace.
- To add comments and hyperlinks to workbooks.

Creating a Template

1 We will first create a template which we can copy and adapt for each car hire branch.

	A	B	C	D	E
1			Profit forecast - 2nd Quarter		
2					
3		Apr	May	Jun	Total
4	No. of Cars				
5	No. of Days	30	31	30	
6	Proportion on hire	0.8	0.85	0.9	
7	Ave. charge per car	30	30	30	
8	Total revenue	0			
9	Running costs per car	0			
10	Depreciation per car	0			
11					
12	Est. operating profit	0			
13					

FIGURE 6.1

2 Enter the following data, using these notes and Figure 6.1 as a guide. Complete rows 4-7 which hold the variables:

Row 4. No. of Cars. Leave this blank as the number of cars for hire will vary between branches/months.

Row 5. The number of days in the month. Enter 30, 31 etc as shown.

Row 6. Proportion on Hire (not every available car is hired). Enter 0.8 (ie 80%) for Apr, 0.85 for May etc as shown.

Row 7. Ave. Charge per Car. This is £30, the average charged per car per day. Enter this for cells B7 to D7. *Do not enter a £ sign.*

The remaining rows are all formulae. Remember that every formula begins with an = sign.

Row 8. Total Revenue is the product of cells B4 to B7, so enter the formula **=B4*B5*B6*B7** in cell **B8**. Until row 4 is completed it will show a value of 0.

Row 9. Running Costs per Car. This is estimated as 15% of Total Revenue (cell B8). Enter **=B8*0.15** in cell **B9**.

Row 10. Depreciation per Car is estimated as 10% of the Total Revenue. Enter **=B8*0.10** in cell **B10**.

Row 12. Estimated Operating Profit is the Total Revenue less Running Costs and Depreciation. Enter **=B8-(B9+B10)** in cell **B12**.

Completing the Worksheet

We need to copy the cell range for the first month across to the other 2 months and then calculate the totals for the quarter. Use Figure 6.2 as a guide.

	A	B	C	D	E
1			Profit forecast - 2nd Quarter		
2					
3		Apr	May	Jun	Total
4	No. of Cars				0
5	No. of Days	30.00	31.00	30.00	91.00
6	Proportion on hire	0.80	0.85	0.90	
7	Ave. charge per car	30.00	30.00	30.00	
8	Total revenue	0.00	0.00	0.00	0.00
9	Running costs per car	0.00	0.00	0.00	0.00
10	Depreciation per car	0.00	0.00	0.00	0.00
11					
12	Est. operating profit	0.00	0.00	0.00	0.00
13					

FIGURE 6.2

1 Select cells **B8** to **D8** and select **EDIT - FILL -RIGHT** option - the formula is copied into cells C8 and D8.
Next select cells **B9** to **D12** and fill right again.

2 Now that we have 3 months of data we can total the 3 months.
Select cell **E5** and click the **AUTOSUM** button (marked with the Sigma symbol, Σ).
Check that cells **B5** to **D5** are outlined and the correct formula **=SUM(B5:D5)** is displayed. Press ENTER and the number of days in the quarter (91) should now be displayed.

(3) Now create the totals for cells **E4**, **E8, E9, E10** and **E12.** The Proportion on Hire and Ave. Charge per Car cannot sensibly be added together.

Note: If you use Autosum with cells E4 and E10 take care; it may identify the incorrect cell range.

(4) Now enter the figure 100 in cell **B4** – Estimated Operating Profit for the quarter should be 54,000. If not check the formula and the data. Erase the entry once you have checked.

(5) **Creating a Template**. If we save the workbook as a template, it will serve as a pattern for future workbooks we will create. We will also create a new folder to store them in.
Select **FILE-SAVE AS**. Choose an appropriate drive/folder and click the **CREATE NEW FOLDER** button.
Name the new folder **Car Hire**.

(6) Select **TEMPLATE** from the **SAVE AS TYPE:** box.
Name the workbook **Forecast Template**.

Note: Excel tries to save all templates in a special template folder; this has the advantage that they are displayed for use on the General tab whenever you create a new workbook. However, we will save our template in the new folder that we have created.

(7) Use the **SAVE IN:** box to select our new folder **Car Hire** – it should be displayed in the **SAVE IN:** box.

(8) Click the **SAVE** button and the workbook is saved as a template file (extension .XLT) in the Car Hire folder. Templates are protected from changes – the user is made to save the amended version as a new workbook.

Copying Templates

You now have a template which can be copied to create workbooks for the 3 car hire branches at Hale, Bowdon and Gatley. We will create 3 copies as ordinary workbooks, plus an extra copy summarising the other three. You can either use **Save As** to save the template under different names, or copy the cell values, formulae etc from the template into a new workbook. We will use the first method.

(1) With the workbook **Forecast Template** open select the options **FILE-SAVE AS**.
In the **FILE NAME** box overtype the current name Forecast Template, with the new name **Hale.**

(2) Check in the **SAVE IN** box that the current folder is **Car Hire**.
In the **SAVE AS TYPE:** box change the file type to **Microsoft Excel Workbook** and click **SAVE**.
The original template workbook is copied as a normal workbook and closed, leaving the new workbook (Hale) displayed.

(3) Repeat the Save As operation to create 3 more workbooks in the same folder – **Bowdon**, **Gatley** and **Summary1**.

(4) Summary1 will be used to summarise the totals in the 3 other workbooks,

so we only need the title and cell labels, not the data and formulae, so we will keep cells **A1** to **E3** – the titles and headings – and **A4** to **A12,** the row labels.
Open Summary1 if necessary and delete the cell range **B4** to **E12**.

5 We now have 4 copies of the original template workbook Forecast Template. They are Hale, Bowdon and Gatley – the 3 car hire branches – and Summary1.
Save and close all the workbooks that remain open, using the **FILE-CLOSE** option.

Locating Workbooks

If your folder structure becomes complex, with many levels of folder and subfolder, it is easy to forget where your workbooks are stored; in this situation Excel's search features help you locate files. This is a good point to try it out.

1 Close any open workbooks. Open the **FILE** menu and select **OPEN**.
The Open dialog box is displayed. Change it to the drive/folder where you have stored the workbooks we created in previous topics (not the Car Hire sub-folder).

2 **File Details**. Click the down arrow next to the **VIEWS** button and select the **DETAILS** option. The full file details given help to identify the correct workbook. Next try the **PROPERTIES** option.

3 **Searching by Workbook Name.** Click the down arrow on the right of the **TOOLS** option and select **FIND**.
Let's locate all the files with the word 'sales' in their name.
Enter *sales* in the **VALUE** box and click the **FIND NOW** button – see Figure 6.3.
Click **YES** on the next dialog box that appears.
Two workbooks are located – **Book Sales** and **Insurance Sales** and could be opened if so desired (this search will obviously only work if they are located in the current folder).

59

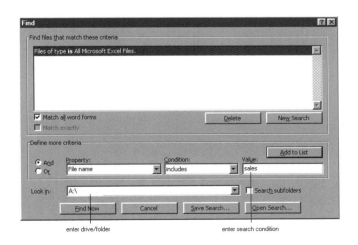

enter drive/folder   enter search condition

FIGURE 6.3

4   **Searching by Workbook Contents.** Select the **FIND** option again. If you can't remember the file name then you can search for files by their contents, eg workbooks that contain data about holidays.
Select the option **TEXT OR PROPERTY** in the **PROPERTY** box and enter the word *Holiday* in the **VALUE** box. Click the **FIND NOW** button.
Click **YES** on the next dialog box that appears.
One workbook is located – **Insurance Sales**.

5   **The Favorites Folder.** The Favorites folder provides a shortcut to a folder that you use often. Try the following:
Make sure that the **FILE-OPEN** dialog box is still displayed and lists the workbooks that you have already created.
Select one but do not open it, eg **Book Sales**.
Now click on the **TOOLS** button and select **ADD TO FAVORITES** button.
Now click the **FAVORITES** button – the **Book Sales** workbook is listed.

6   **The My Documents Folder (information only).** This folder is provided for you to store current work. It is located in the root folder of the hard drive, eg C:\My Documents. When you first use the **OPEN** or **SAVE AS** commands in an Excel session it is the default folder. This folder can soon get very full if it is used indiscriminately, especially if several users of a PC all use it.

7   Cancel the **OPEN** dialog box.

Handling Multiple Workbooks

1   Open the 4 workbooks **Hale**, **Bowdon**, **Gatley** and **Summary1**. They are probably listed at the bottom of the File menu if they were the last workbooks used.

2   **Displaying Multiple Workbooks.** You can display the 4 workbook windows on screen in different ways using the Window-Arrange menu.
Open the **WINDOW** menu – all the open workbooks are listed – and select **ARRANGE** then **TILED**.
The workbooks are arranged side by side – see Figure 6.4. It doesn't matter if your workbooks are in a different order to this.

FIGURE 6.4

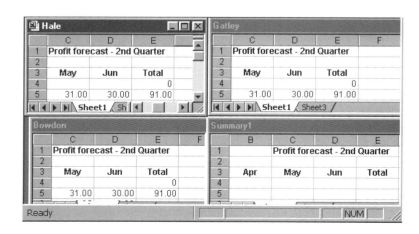

Select each workbook in turn – it becomes the active workbook with the Title Bar in blue.

3 Now for each workbook enter the number of cars for each car hire branch in row 4 as follows:

	Apr	May	Jun
Hale	25	32	40
Bowdon	32	40	60
Gatley	41	36	60

Linking Formulae

1 We will use a formula in the summary workbook to add together the contents of cell B4 for the 3 branches. This involves 'external' references. Select cell **B4** in the **Summary1** workbook.
Enter the formula = **Bowdon.XLS!B4+Gatley.XLS!B4+Hale.XLS!B4** in this cell.
The number of cars for April at the 3 car hire branches is placed in cell B4 in workbook **Summary1**. The total should be 98 – if not check the data in the 3 other workbooks and the above formula.

2 *Notes:* The linking formula uses external references to 3 different workbooks. Each external reference must consist of:

▓ the full name of the external workbook
▓ the cell reference
▓ both separated by an exclamation mark.

If more than one sheet in a workbook is used then the sheet name should be included too. If the formula is correctly entered Excel adds brackets around the three external cell references and inserts the sheet names for you.

3 **Copying Linking Formulae**. Maximise the **Summary1** workbook.
Select cell range **B4** to **D4**, and use the **EDIT-FILL-RIGHT** command to copy the formula to cells **C4** and **D4**.
Select cell range **B4** to **D12** and select **EDIT-FILL-DOWN**.
Select cell range **B6** to **D7** and delete their contents. Rows 6 and 7 – the Proportion on Hire and Ave Charge per car cannot be added together. Similarly delete the three totals in row 11.

4 You can also create the totals in column **E** using the **EDIT-FILL-RIGHT** command.
Format the cell range **B8** to **E12** to include commas and zero decimal places using the **FORMAT-CELLS** command or the comma button on the Formatting Toolbar.

Note: If a cell displays #### symbols the column is too narrow and needs widening.

5 Check your totals with Figure 6.5 below.
Use **WINDOW-ARRANGE** to show the 4 workbooks in tiled display again.

	A	B	C	D	E	F
1		Overall Profit forecast - 2nd Quarter				
2						
3		Apr	May	Jun	Total	
4	No. of Cars	98	108	160	366	
5	No. of Days	90	93	90	273	
6	Proportion on hire					
7	Ave. charge per car					
8	Total revenue	70,560	85,374	129,600	285,534	
9	Running costs per car	10,584	12,806	19,440	42,830	
10	Depreciation per car	7,056	8,537	12,960	28,553	
11						
12	Est. operating profit	52,920	64,031	97,200	214,151	
13						

FIGURE 6.5

6 Changes made to any of the three supporting workbooks – **Bowdon**, **Hale**, or **Gatley** – will be reflected in the summary or dependent workbook **Summary1**.
Try the two following 'what if' experiments:

(a) At the moment the three branches overall Total Operating Profit for April is £59,920. The target is £60,000. Amend the Ave. Charge per Car for April (**B7**) to 35 for each of the three supporting workbooks.
Activate the **Summary 1** workbook and check cell **B12** – the target is now achieved.

(b) The Proportion on Hire for June for Hale Branch drops to 80% (amend cell **D6** on the **Hale** workbook to 0.8) – will the quarter's estimated operating profit still exceed £220,000 for the three car hire branches?
Now look at cell **E12** in the **Summary1** workbook – the target is still achieved.

(c) Undo these 2 sets of changes using the **EDIT-UNDO** option.

Creating a Workspace File

At the moment we have 3 workbooks linked to a summary 'dependent' workbook by external formulae; if we were to close the summary workbook first and continued using the other 3 there is a danger that any changes in them might not be reflected in the summary. If you save the group of 4 workbooks as a 'workspace' then they become easy to save and retrieve as a group. Excel will also remember the relative arrangements and sizes of each workbook window on screen.

1 Arrange the 4 workbooks in tiled display.

2 Select the options **FILE-SAVE WORKSPACE**. Replace the default name **RESUME** with the workspace name **Branch Profits** and before you save it check that it will be stored in the folder **Car Hire** along with the other 4 workbooks.
The workspace Branch Profits – extension .XLW – is now created.

Note: If you have saved the workbooks and workspace files to diskette it will take some time to save all the links.

3 Exit Excel, saving the workbooks if necessary.

(4) Start Excel again and open the **FILE** menu; check at the bottom of the menu items – you should see the workbooks listed individually as well as the workspace file **Group Profits**. The workbooks can still be opened individually.
Open the supporting workbook **Bowdon**.
Amend the Proportion on Hire for May to 0.82.
Save and close the workbook.

(5) Now open the **Summary1** workbook and a message appears, asking you if you wish to update links. Click **YES** – check that the totals for May are updated to reflect the changes made in the supporting workbook **Bowdon**.

(6) Save and close the workbook **Summary1**.

Linking External Ranges with Paste Link

In previous tasks we have linked workbooks using external references to cells in other workbooks. We can achieve the same result using the Paste Link command. Paste link ensures that when the original cells change the pasted copy changes too. We will use this when we will copy some totals from the Summary 1 workbook to a new workbook.

(1) Open the workbook **Summary1** again and maximise it if necessary. If you are prompted to update links do so.

(2) Open a new blank workbook and save it as **Summary2** – check that you save it in the **Car Hire** folder along with the other four related workbooks. **Summary2** will hold the summaries of the operating profits for the quarter.

(3) Select **WINDOW-ARRANGE-CASCADE** and click the edge of **Summary1** to place it on top.

(4) Select cells **A8** to **E8** and copy them using **EDIT-COPY**.
Now select cell **A3** in workbook **Summary2**.
Select the **EDIT-PASTE SPECIAL** command and click the **PASTE LINK** button in the dialog box that appears.
When the cells are copied from **Summary1** to **Summary2** check the linking formula in the Formula Bar.

(5) Now repeat **PASTE-LINK** twice more to copy rows **9** to **12** from the **Summary1** workbook to rows **4** to **7** respectively of the **Summary2** workbook.

(6) Check that the figures are the same in the two workbooks, then format the Summary2 workbook.

(7) Save and close both workbooks.

(8) To test the new links open the workbook **Hale** and amend the the number of cars for June to 45. Save and close the workbook.

(9) Open the workbook **Summary1**. If you are prompted to update links do so and note down the grand total in cell **E12** – it is updated by the changes you have made to the supporting workbook, Hale.

(10) Open the workbook **Summary2** and note the grand total – it has been changed in turn by the updating of Summary 1.

Comments and Hyperlinks

Comments are useful as notes or reminders to explain the workbook – either to yourself or to co-workers. Hyperlinks are extensively used in Windows-based applications, eg in Help or Web pages, to 'jump' from one location to another. They can also be used to link to other cells, another workbook or Office document, or to a Web page. We will use them to link two workbooks.

(1) **Adding Comments.** Using the workbook **Summary2** select **FILE-PROPERTIES-SUMMARY**. Add a title, subject and short summary of the workbook to the summary dialog box.

Note: You can use **SAVE PREVIEW PICTURE** to preview a workbook before opening it; this is useful for large files that take a long time to load.

(2) **Cell Comments**. Using the **Summary1** workbook right click cell **B13** and select **INSERT COMMENT**.
Add a comment to the box, eg, *'Based on operating profits for rooms and food at the Hale, Bowdon and Gatley branches.'*
De-select the comment box. The mark in the cell corner shows that you can view a comment whenever the screen pointer rests on the cell (to delete a comment right click the cell and choose Delete).

(3) **Hyperlinks**. We wish to link cell A12 in workbook **Summary1** with the equivalent cell in the **Summary2** workbook – A7.
Right click cell **A12** and select **HYPERLINK**. A dialog box appears.
Click the **FILE** button and the **LINK TO FILE** dialog box opens. Select Summary2 from the list and click **OK**.
Now click the **BOOKMARK** button and the dialog box **SELECT PLACE IN DOCUMENT** appears. Select **Sheet1** and type in the cell reference **A7**.
Click **OK** on both dialog boxes.

(4) The text in cell A12 of **Summary1** is now coloured blue, indicating a hyperlink.
Click the cell and you are taken to the equivalent row in the **Summary2** workbook.

(5) Create a hyperlink in cell **A7** of the **Summary2** workbook to return you to the starting cell in Summary1.

Input and Lookup Tables

Introduction

You can create various types of data tables in Excel. In this topic we will be creating two types:

Input Tables are generated from data based on variables and formulae. In Figure 7.1 an input table of loan repayments is built up from a column of various interest rates.

Lookup Tables work in the opposite way to input tables; you use a special function to look up values in a table that has already been created. In Figure 7.7 the table is used to calculate sales commissions.

Topic Objectives

- To create a data series.
- To use cell names in formulae.
- To create one-input and two-input tables.
- To use the PMT function to calculate loan interest.
- To create a lookup table.

Creating One-input Tables

In other topics we have tried substituting different values in a formula to see their effect. Once this range of values gets larger it is quicker to use a data table.

1   The simplest type is a one-input table which holds values for one variable; in this case interest rates.
Create the worksheet shown in Figure 7.1, using a new workbook. Format it as shown.
Enter 6.00% in cell **A9** – enter the percentage sign too.

	A	B
1		Table of Loan Repayments
2		
3	Repayment term in months	60
4	Interest Rate	8%
5	Loan Amount	5000
6		
7	Possible Interest Rate:	Monthly Repayment
8		
9		6.00%
10		6.25%
11		6.50%
12		6.75%
13		7.00%
14		7.25%
15		7.50%
16		7.75%
17		8.00%

FIGURE 7.1

2 We will use a data series to enter the percentages in column A. Select the options **EDIT-FILL-SERIES**.

Enter the values in the dialog box, using Figure 7.2 as a guide.

FIGURE 7.2

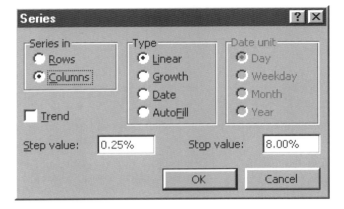

3 Enter the interest rate, repayment term and loan amount as shown in Figure 7.1.

Use **FORMAT-CELLS-BORDER** to outline cell **B8** where the result will appear.

Save the workbook as **Loan Table**.

4 **Naming Cells.** We can name cells and use these names in formulae rather than cell references - see note below.

Select cell **B4**, and select **INSERT - NAME -DEFINE**. In the dialog box overtype the default name with the name **RATE**, then click **OK**. Similarly name cell **B3 TERM**, and name cell **B5 AMOUNT**.

Notes: It can be easier to use cell names in formulae rather than their references. The Name box to the left of the Formula Bar shows all the names used in the workbook. You can insert cell names into formula by selecting them from this name box.

5 **The PMT Function.** The PMT function is used to calculate payments made at regular intervals at fixed interest rates, such as loans or mortgages.

The syntax is **=PMT(interest,term,principal)** where interest is the interest rate, term is the repayment term, and principal the amount borrowed (see Help for more information).

In cell **B8** enter the formula **=PMT(rate/12,term,-amount)**

The monthly repayment of 101.38 is now displayed in cell B8; it is based on the values in cell range **B3** to **B5**.

Notes: Rate is divided by 12 to give the monthly repayment and the − sign converts the result to a positive rather than a negative number. If your formula is not correct then check the cell data, names and the formula.

6 **One-input Tables.** We can now create a table in cells A9 to B17, based on the interest rates we have entered. This will let us see the effect on the monthly repayments of various interest rates.

Select cell range **A8** to **B17**.

66

Select the **DATA-TABLE** option.
In the dialog box enter the cell reference **B4** in the **COLUMN INPUT CELL** box and click **OK**.

(7) Cell range A8 to B17 is an input table and cell B4 is the cell where different interest rates can be entered.
Different monthly repayments, based on different rates of interest, are now shown in cells **B9** to **B17,** and can be compared with the repayment figure in cell B8.
Use the **FORMAT-CELLS-NUMBER** to format the table entries to 2 decimal places. Your table should now look like Figure 7.3 below.

	A	B
1		Table of Loan Repayments
2		
3	Repayment term in months	60
4	Interest Rate	8%
5	Loan Amount	5000
6		
7	Possible Interest Rate:	Monthly Repayment
8		£101.38
9	6.00%	96.66
10	6.25%	97.25
11	6.50%	97.83
12	6.75%	98.42
13	7.00%	99.01
14	7.25%	99.60
15	7.50%	100.19
16	7.75%	100.78
17	8.00%	101.38

FIGURE 7.3

(8) Amend the interest rate to 6%, and the loan amount to 7000.
The new repayment is shown in cell B8 – 135.33 per month. The other repayments in the input table cells are also re-calculated.
At what interest rate would you start to pay more than £150 per month?

(9) **Extending the One-input Table.**
We will create another table showing how the interest rate affects the total cost of the loan. The total cost is the monthly repayment multiplied by the period of the loan, as shown in Figure 7.4 below.
Enter the label *Total Repaid* in cell **C7**.
Enter the formula **=B8*TERM** in cell **C8**. Format this cell to 2 decimal places and insert commas.
Select the cell range **A8** to **C17** (the new table range).
Select the **DATA-TABLE** options and enter the cell reference **B4** in the **COLUMN INPUT CELL** box.
The second table is created in column C, showing the total amount repaid over the period of the loan.

(10) Format the table values and place a border around cell **C8**.

	A	B	C
1		Table of Loan Repayments	
2			
3	Repayment term in months	60	
4	Interest Rate	6%	
5	Loan Amount	7000	
6			
7	Possible Interest Rate:	Monthly Repayment	Total Repaid
8		£135.33	8119.78
9	6.00%	135.33	8119.78
10	6.25%	136.14	8168.69
11	6.50%	136.96	8217.78
12	6.75%	137.78	8267.05
13	7.00%	138.61	8316.50
14	7.25%	139.44	8366.13
15	7.50%	140.27	8415.94
16	7.75%	141.10	8465.92
17	8.00%	141.93	8516.09

FIGURE 7.4

(11) Alter the interest rate to 7.5%, the term to 72, and the amount borrowed to 10,000.

(a) What is the total amount repaid?

(b) What is the monthly repayment?

Two-input Tables

The one-input tables we have just created are both based around one variable, the interest rate, ie they are one dimensional. A two-input table uses two variables; the one we are going to create, shown in Figure 7.5, uses purchase amount and discount rate to calculate discount, eg purchases up to £10,000 get a 5% discount rate.

	A	B	C	D	E	F	G
1			Discount Table				
2							
3							
4				Discount Rates			
5							
6			5%	7%	9%	11%	13%
7		10000					
8		15000					
9	Purchase Amount	20000					
10		25000					
11		30000					
12							

FIGURE 7.5

(1) Enter the information shown in Figure 7.5 in a new workbook. Format it as shown – use the Drawing Toolbar to draw the arrows.
Save the workbook as **Discount**.

(2) The discount given is the discount rate multiplied by the amount purchased.
The formula must be entered where the row and column variables intersect – cell B6.

Enter the formula **=B3*B4** in cell **B6**.

Note: Cells B3 and B4 have been chosen for the above formula but these cells will be left blank as the two-input table generates all the values we need. Unlike the one-input table we don't need to enter the second variable. As the table needs to use two cells when it calculates we use B3 and B4, but any empty cells outside the table will do.

3 Now select cell range **B6** to **G11** – these are the cells that the table will fill. Select **DATA-TABLE** and enter **B3** in the **ROW INPUT CELL** box and **B4** in the **COLUMN INPUT CELL** box.

The discount table is created, showing 25 separate calculations – it should now look like Figure 7.6. The alternative would be to enter all them all as separate formulae, but this is obviously far quicker.

	A	B	C	D	E	F	G
1			Discount Table				
2							
3							
4				Discount Rates			
5							
6		0	5%	7%	9%	11%	13%
7		10000	500	700	900	1100	1300
8		15000	750	1050	1350	1650	1950
9	Purchase Amount	20000	1000	1400	1800	2200	2600
10		25000	1250	1750	2250	2750	3250
11		30000	1500	2100	2700	3300	3900
12							
13	Enter number of weeks:						

FIGURE 7.6

4 **Consolidation.** The present table represents discount on goods purchased by customers in a weekly period. It is an easy matter to adapt it to calculate it for any number of weeks.
Enter the label in cell **A13** shown in Figure 7.6. above.
Change the formula in cell **B6** so that it includes cell **B13**, ie **=B3*B4*B13**
Now enter 8 in cell **B13** – the table is recalculated, showing the discount for 8 weeks at various discount rates.

5 **Notes on input tables.**
To delete a table select the whole table and then use **EDIT-CUT** or **CLEAR** or press the **DELETE** key.
To modify a table select the whole table and select **DATA-TABLE**.
To extend the range of a table first enter the extra values then modify it as above.

Creating Lookup Tables

One and two-input tables are based on formula and one or more variables input by the user. Lookup tables use the opposite approach – the table values are already created and are looked up using variables entered in another part of the worksheet. Look at the worksheet in Figure 7.7 below. In columns E to G is a table to look up commission, based on the sale value – from £0 to £8,000 – and the type of sale (cash or credit). As the commission rates in the table do not follow a regular numeric sequence, we could not generate them by using a formula.

	A	B	C	D	E	F	G
1					Commission Look-up Table		
2							
3	Cash Sale						
4	Amount of Sale						
5	Commission				Amount of Sale	Cash	Credit
6					0	5%	0%
7	Credit Sale				500	8%	5%
8	Amount of Sale				1000	10%	8%
9	Commission				4000	15%	10%
10					8000	20%	15%
11							

There are two table lookup functions, HLOOKUP and VLOOKUP:

HLOOKUP is for values arranged horizontally in a row.
The function is **=HLOOKUP(x,range,index)**.
VLOOKUP is for values arranged vertically in a column, as they are in Figure 7.7. This is the usual arrangement. The function is **=VLOOKUP(x,range,index)**.

- **x** is the value that you want to look up in the table (text, number, or a cell reference)
- **range** is the cells making up the table
- **index** is the reference of the columns or rows to look in.

In the example shown in Figure 7.7:

- **x** is cell **B4** where the value of the sale is entered
- **range** is the lookup table, cell range **E6** to **G10**
- **index** are columns F and G holding the lookup values.

Note: The LOOKUP function will not work unless the first column of the lookup table (column E) holds entries that look up items in immediately adjacent columns (column F and G). Entries must be unique and in ascending order.

1 Enter the data shown in Figure 7.7 in a new workbook. Enter 800 in cell **B4**.

2 Enter the formula **=VLOOKUP(B4,E6:G10,2)** in cell **B5**.

3 *Notes*: Enter the formula in lower case – if correctly entered Excel converts it to upper case.
The formula means 'look up the value in cell B4, from the table in cell range E6 to G10, in the 2nd column of the table'.
The Vlookup function searches the first column of compare values – column E – until it reaches a number equal to or higher than 800 (cell E8). It then goes back a row if it is higher (to cell E7), then goes to the second column (F) and looks up the commission of 8% (in cell F7). For this reason the values in the first column of the table – column D – must be in ascending order.

4 The commission is displayed in cell B5 as 0.08. Use the **FORMAT-CELLS-NUMBER** command and select **PERCENTAGE** from the category list and 0 from decimal places box. The commission is now displayed as 8%.

5 Repeat these operations to enter another VLOOKUP formula in cell **B9** calculating the commission on credit orders.
Note: You should modify the cell reference for the lookup value (B8) and the column number (3) where the lookup values are held.

6 Enter a credit order value of 7,000 in cell B8. Check that the commission is 10%.

7 Save the workbook as **Commission Table**.

Analysis Tools – Goal Seek and Solver

Introduction

Excel offers two special analysis tools – Goal Seek and Solver. We have already used Goal Seek in charts in Topic 4; it is the simpler of the two tools, allowing you to alter one variable to achieve a particular value, eg to amend sales figures to achieve a particular profit. Solver is more complex to use and can handle a large number of interdependent variables, as we will see.

First check that they are installed on the **TOOLS** menu; if not then they may be listed under the **ADD-INS** option – also on the Tools menu. If not then you will need the Excel 2000 installation disk.

Topic Objectives

- To use Goal Seek to reach a target value for a variable.
- To use Solver to handle multiple constraints and variables.
- To save Solver results in Scenario Manager.
- To print scenarios in Report Manager.

Goal Seek

1 Goal Seek will change the value of a variable until a formula achieves a desired value. Open the workbook **Gatley**. It is in the folder **Car Hire**. You will recall from Topic 6 that it estimates the quarterly operating profit for a car hire company.

We want to find out what proportion of cars on hire in May would achieve a total operating profit of £23,000 for this month. Instead of trial and error – amending the 'Proportion on Hire' cell (C6) to observe the effects – we can use Goal Seek.

2 Select **TOOLS-GOAL SEEK** – a dialog box appears.

Note: You can use the Collapse button, located next to the data entry boxes, to reduce the size of the dialog box and see the effects of Goal Seek.

FIGURE 8.1

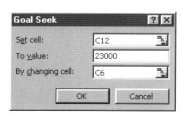

3   Complete the box using Figure 8.1 as a guide, ie:

Set cell	**C12**
To value	**23000**
By changing cell	**C6**

Note the present value of cell C6.
Click **OK** and a second dialog box reports the solution.
The value of cell C6 is changed to 0.92 – the proportion on hire needed to achieve the £23,000 goal.

4   Click the **CANCEL** button to restore the original value of cell C6 and any related cells.

Note: If you click **OK** by accident then use **EDIT-UNDO**.

5   Try the following Goal Seek; what average charge per car for April would achieve a total car revenue of £85,000?

6   **Consolidation.** (optional) Open the workbook **Budget** created in Topic 1 and select the worksheet **Spring Term**.
How large a student loan would you need in week 9 to achieve a closing balance of £342 in week 9?

7   Close the workbooks **Gatley** and **Budget** without saving any changes.

8   **Notes on Goal Seek.**

(a) The Goal Seek Status dialog box has two further buttons:
PAUSE – allows you to pause during a lengthy goal seek.
STEP – allows you to seek one step at a time if you want to gradually narrow down the goal seek.

(b) Goal Seek will not work if the cell whose value you try to set contains a formula, it must contain a value.

(c) The cell whose value you wish to set must be linked by a formula(e) to the cell whose target value you are changing.

(d) You can also goal seek by 'dragging' chart data – see Topic 4.

Using Solver

Goal Seek can achieve a target value by substituting various values for a variable, but it cannot deal with a range of interacting variables or work out what the optimum combination is. This is Solver's special strength, it can juggle a number of interdependent variables and arrive at a 'best fit' solution, eg scheduling employees to keep labour costs down, maximising income from a range of investments, or choosing the best delivery routes. It uses a combination of iterations and algebraic techniques to converge on the optimum solution. You can place constraints on the maximum and minimum values of certain variables, eg hours worked per week. However, Solver needs to be used with caution; if the problem is a complex one then the problem – the range of values, contraints, etc that you have specified – may have more than one solution (or no solution). You need to be aware of this and perhaps run Solver more than once, changing the parameters, rather than give up or accept a possibly misleading solution.

FIGURE 8.2

	A	B	C	D	E
1			New Magazines - Profit Forecast		
2					
3					
4			Number	Profit per	Profit (£)
5			Printed	Magazine (£)	
6	Model Yachting		3000	1.30	3900
7	60's Sounds		2000	1.00	2000
8	Scooter Rider		1500	1.60	2400
9	Totals		6500		8300
10					

1   Our Solver problem is based around magazine publishing – see Figure 8.2. The figures in the worksheet show the marketing department's current sales and profit predictions. The publishing company wants to make a profit of £9,000 for three new magazines, subject to the following 4 constraints, which are based on maximum production capacity, distribution constraints and predicted market demand:
It must print at least 3000 copies of 'Model Yachting'.
It cannot print more than 2500 of '60's Sounds' and 1800 of 'Scooter Rider'.
Overall production of the three magazines can rise to a maximum of no more than 7000.

2   Total columns C and E down, and multiply the values in rows 6 to 8 across to calculate the profit forecasts shown in column E.
Save the workbook as **Profit Forecast**.

3   Open the **TOOLS** menu and select **SOLVER**. If Solver does not start then it will need to be installed – see above.
The Solver Parameters dialog box appears.

FIGURE 8.3

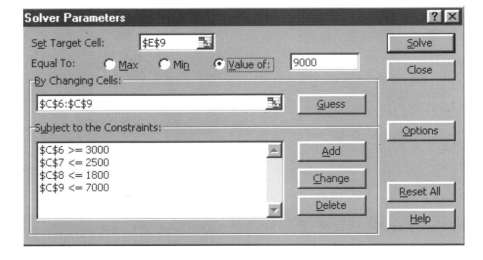

Complete the first part of the dialog box as follows – Figure 8.3 shows the completed parameters.

Note: Solver converts the cell references to absolute references.

Set Target Cell: **Enter E9**

Equal to buttons: Make sure that **Value of** is selected and 9000
entered as shown.

4 Click the **BY CHANGING CELLS** box and enter **C6:C9** (we want to vary the
number of each magazine printed and the total magazines printed).

5 We must apply the 4 constraints mentioned above now:

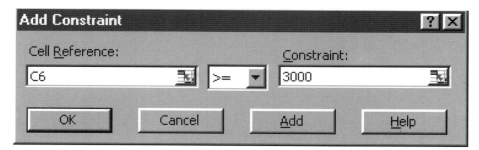

FIGURE 8.4

Click the **ADD** button and a new dialog box appears – **ADD
CONSTRAINT**.
Add the following constraints using Figure 8.4 as a guide.
Insert the cell references **C6** in the **CELL REFERENCE** box.
Set the relationship to **>=** in the middle box.
Finally click the **CONSTRAINT** box and insert 3000.
Click **OK** and you are returned to the Solver Parameters dialog box. The
constraint is shown – **$C$6>=3000**

Note: If you have made an error then click either the **CHANGE** button to
edit it, or the **DELETE** button and start again.

6 Add the second constraint, following the same steps as before. The
constraint is **C7<=2500** (ie the number of '60's Sounds' magazine must not
exceed 2500).
Enter the 2 remaining parameters and compare the completed dialog box
with Figure 8.4 above. Cancel the **ADD CONSTRAINT** box if necessary.

7 Click the **SOLVE** button and Solver makes a series of 'tries' or iterations
based on the target value and the constraints entered. If you have input
them correctly it finds a valid solution and modifies the figures in the
worksheet.
Move the Results dialog box aside so that you can see the solution. Solver
has worked out how many of each magazine need to be printed to achieve
the profit of £9000.

8 **Solver Reports**. You are offered the option of keeping the Solver solution
or restoring the original values; select **RESTORE ORIGINAL VALUES**
then select the **ANSWER** option in the **REPORTS** box and click **OK**.
The report is generated as a separate worksheet – **Answer Report1**. You
will see that it summarises the Solver data, ie:

  the value of the target cell **E9**
  the values reached for the adjustable cells **C6:C9**

how well the constraints were met:
Binding – the cell value equals the constraint value,
Not Binding – the constraint was met but Solver could not find an equal value,
Not Satisfied – would mean that the constraint value could not be met.

(9) Run Solver again. When the **SOLVER RESULTS** dialog box is displayed click the **SAVE SCENARIO** button.
Save the scenario as **Profits1** then click **OK.**
You are returned to the Solver Results dialog box.
Click the **RESTORE ORIGINAL VALUES** option then click **OK**.

(10) Now save the workbook – the most recent Solver settings are saved too.
Carry straight on with the next task.

Using Scenario Manager

In the previous task you have saved a Solver solution as a scenario. Scenario Manager allows you to save such combinations of variables as named scenarios; you can then view them, change them and print reports showing alternative scenarios.
Note: You can also use Scenario Manager with Goal Seek or manually generated variables.

(1) **Running a Scenario**. Select the **TOOLS-SCENARIOS** option. Move the dialog box to one side so that you can see the scenario values.
Select the scenario **Profits1** and click **SHOW**. The Solver solution is applied and the cell values change.
Close the Scenario Manager dialog box – the scenario values remain assigned to the cells.

(2) **Printing Scenarios using Report Manager**.

(a) Select the **VIEW-REPORT MANAGER** option. If it is not shown on the View menu it will need to be installed – see above.
Click the **ADD** button on the Report Manager dialog box.

(b) Enter the Report Name *Profits1 Report* in the Add Report dialog box that appears.

(c) Click the down arrow on the **SCENARIO** box – it is in the **SECTION TO ADD** section.
Select the scenario **Profits1** and click **ADD**.

(d) The scenario is added to the report – click **OK** and the Report Manager dialog box appears.

(e) Click the **PRINT** button. The printed report will contain the set of values generated by Solver in the previous activity.

Note: Printing. Report Manager can save you a lot of time if you have saved a number of scenarios and wish to print them all off at once.

Excel Functions

Introduction

We cannot cover all the Excel functions in this topic; there are over 200 and many, such as trigonometric, engineering and financial functions, require specialised knowledge to use. Some functions we have already used, such as the simpler maths functions in Topic 1 and the database functions in Topic 5. In the first task in this topic we will briefly review the various types of functions and we will then try out some of the commoner ones in the remaining tasks.

Topic Objectives

- To review the range of Excel Functions.
- To perform date calculations.
- To use the logical function IF.
- To use statistical functions MAX, MIN, AVERAGE, STDEV, FORECAST and TREND.
- To use the financial functions Future Value and Straight Line Depreciation.
- To use Paste Function to enter function arguments.

The Range of Excel Functions

Notes on Using Functions

- Functions are predefined formulae that perform standard calculations.
- A function is part of a formula and must start with an = sign.
- You can enter functions in either lower or upper case. If you type functions in lower case Excel will convert it to upper case if you have typed it correctly.
- A function should contain no spaces.
- Excel's Paste Function feature lets you choose the function from a list and paste it into a cell. This is useful for complex or unusual functions.
- The information you supply for the function to work is called *arguments*, eg AVERAGE(range) needs you to supply the *cell range* argument.
- Function arguments are enclosed in parentheses – the standard round brackets – (). You must type these yourself. Optional arguments are shown in the Help text in square brackets – [ ]. These are for your guidance only and should **not** be typed.
- Often a function uses two or more arguments; you must separate them by commas.

1 **Functions Types.** Open a new workbook and open the Paste Function dialog box. You can either use the **INSERT-FUNCTION** option or the **PASTE FUNCTION** button (marked 'fx' on the Standard Toolbar).

Eleven types of function are listed. If the Office Assistant opens as well read section 3 below – you can use it for extra guidance in this task if you wish.

Select the Function Category – **MOST RECENTLY USED**. The **FUNCTION NAME** box lists functions we have used recently. Select each function and a brief explanation and syntax are given.

The second function category **ALL** lists all the Excel functions – try this.

2 Now review the rest of the Function categories:

Financial and **Date and Time** functions are used in the next task.

Mathematical and **Trigonometric** are eg, square roots and cosines etc plus functions such as SUM.

Statistical functions calculate such things as average and standard deviation; we use these in the next task.

Lookup and Reference functions were used in Topic 7 for lookup tables.

Database functions operate on database records, eg averaging certain types of record – see Topic 5.

Text functions act on text information, eg finding the length of a string of text or converting it to upper case.

Logical functions test certain conditions and return a TRUE or FALSE answer. We use the IF function in the next task.

Information functions test cells for certain conditions or contents, eg error messages or blank cells.

3 **Office Assistant.** When you open the Paste Function dialog box the Office Assistant may also be displayed. If it is not and you want to use it then click the **OFFICE ASSISTANT** button. It is at the bottom left of the dialog box, marked with a '?'. If it has not been installed or you don't want to use Office Assistant's help with functions then go to section 4.

(a) Click on **FINANCIAL** functions and select the **FV** function.

(b) Select the Office Assistant option 'help with this feature' and click the **HELP ON SELECTED FUNCTION** button.

(c) The Future Value function is explained in the Help text.
Close the Help window then the Office Assistant window using the ? button.

(d) *Note*: At stage (b) it is also possible to enter a natural language description eg 'find the minimum value in a database' and click the **SEARCH** button. Office Assistant should suggest one or two functions, including the correct one DMIN. Natural language searches depend heavily on your skill in using appropriate search terms to narrow down the search to the function that you require. If for example you use the term 'lowest' instead of 'minimum' the search doesn't work as well. If you prefer you can enter keywords rather than a whole phrase, eg 'database' and 'minimum'.

4 Cancel the Paste Function dialog box now.

Using Functions

	A	B	C	D	E	F
1			Share Performance		30-Apr-00	
2						
3	Date	Major	Newsome	Sutton	Overall Change	Increase or
4		Holdings	Group	Engineering	for 3 Companies	Decrease?
5	03-Apr	29.33	60.58	81.98		
6	04-Apr	29.33	61.32	81.98		
7	05-Apr	30.65	61.32	84.67		
8	06-Apr	30.50	62.00	83.65		
9	07-Apr	29.47	62.76	83.66		
10	10-Apr	31.00	63.72	83.41		
11	11-Apr	31.56	64.00	82.45		
12	12-Apr	31.85	65.49	85.85		
13	13-Apr	30.67	64.96	88.00		
14	14-Apr	30.44	62.00	88.17		
15						
16	Hi Val					
17	Lo Val					
18	Av. Value					
19	Std. Dev.					

FIGURE 9.1

① Figure 9.1 shows the performance of three company shares over a 10 day period. We will use it to try out a range of useful functions.

② **The Date Function.** Open a new workbook and enter the formula **=NOW()** in cell **E1**.
A row of hash symbols (###) indicates that the column is too narrow. Format it to a date-only format using the **FORMAT**-**CELLS**-**NUMBER** options.
Complete the rest of the worksheet data shown in Figure 9.1, formatting cell range **B5** to **D19** to 2 decimal places.

③ Rows 16 to 18 will display the maximum, minimum and average value of the three shares over the 10 day period. Row 19 will show the standard deviation, ie the amount by which share prices have deviated from the average.
In cell **B16** enter the function **=MAX(B5:B14)**
In cell **B17** enter the function **=MIN(B5:B14)**

④ Enter a formula for the **AVERAGE** function in cell **B18** and a formula for the **STDEV** function in cell **B19**.

⑤ Copy these functions to columns C and D using the **EDIT-FILL-RIGHT** command.

⑥ Columns E and F will show how the value of the three shares have changed in value over 10 days.
In cell **E5** add up the values for the three shares on the opening date (cell range **B5** to **D5)**.
Do the same for the last date 14-Apr, in cell **E14**.
Compare your worksheet with Figure 9.2 now.

	A	B	C	D	E	F
1			Share Performance		30-Apr-00	
2						
3	Date	Major	Newsome	Sutton	Overall Change	Increase or
4		Holdings	Group	Engineering	for 3 Companies	Decrease?
5	03-Apr	29.33	60.58	81.98	171.89	
6	04-Apr	29.33	61.32	81.98		
7	05-Apr	30.65	61.32	84.67		
8	06-Apr	30.50	62.00	83.65		
9	07-Apr	29.47	62.76	83.66		
10	10-Apr	31.00	63.72	83.41		
11	11-Apr	31.56	64.00	82.45		
12	12-Apr	31.85	65.49	85.85		
13	13-Apr	30.67	64.96	88.00		
14	14-Apr	30.44	62.00	88.17	180.61	
15						
16	Hi Val	31.85	65.49	88.17		
17	Lo Val	29.33	60.58	81.98		
18	Av. Value	30.48	62.82	84.38		
19	Std. Dev.	0.88	1.66	2.28		

FIGURE 9.2

7 To monitor whether the shares have shown an overall increase or decrease we can use the logical function **IF()** and display an appropriate message. In cell **F14** enter the formula =**IF(E14>E5,"share increase","share decrease")**

Now test the IF function by changing the value of cell **C14** to 40.

If the function is correct the message will change to 'share decrease' because the IF condition has become false. Restore the original cell value and the 'share increase' message is displayed.

8 **Calculating with Dates.** In Excel you can calculate with dates, eg they can be added and subtracted. You do not necessarily need a function for all date calculations. We will calculate the number of days between the earliest and latest dates.

Enter the label *'Time in Days'* in cell **G14**.

Enter the formula =**A14-A5** in cell **H14**. The number of days is calculated as 11. If necessary format the cell to a whole number.

9 Save the workbook as **Share Performance**.

10 **Financial Functions.** Try out the following financial functions in a new worksheet:

(a) **Future Value:** If we invest £1000 every year at 7% annual interest what is the investment worth in 5 years?

Enter the following formula =**FV(7%,5,-1000)** – your investment after 5 years is worth £5750.74.

(b) **Straight Line Depreciation:** If we buy a car for £1000 it may only be worth £200 in 5 years. We will use Paste Function to calculate the annual depreciation ('straight line' implies that the rate of depreciation is constant).

Select **INSERT-FUNCTION** and select **FINANCIAL** from the Function Category box and **SLN** from the Function name box.

Click **OK** button – try to enter the arguments for yourself in the second dialog box. As each box is selected the 'argument' that you need to enter is explained and the result of the formula predicted. The annual depreciation should be £160.00.

Trend and Forecast Functions

Forecast and Trend are Excel statistical functions that predict trends using existing data as a basis. Many types of trend can be predicted in this way, eg sales, commodity prices and goods in stock.

1 Open the workbook **Book Sales**. Sheet1 records book sales and revenue for June to October. We will use the Forecast function to predict November sales. However as the function requires numeric data we must change the months in column A to numbers – see Figure 9.3.
Enter 6 in cell **A9**.

	A	B	C	D
1			Book Sales	
2				
3	Month	No. Sold	Revenue	Advertising
4	1	730	1990	180
5	2	890	3030	305
6	3	1055	3440	380
7	4	1310	4421	640
8	5	1600	5029	690
9	6			

FIGURE 9.3

81

2 Click cell **B9**. Select **INSERT-FUNCTION** and select **STATISTICAL** from the Function Category box and **FORECAST** from the Function name box. Click **OK** and enter the arguments as shown in Figure 9.4 in the second dialog box.
Click the **OK** button and the sales forecast for month 6 is shown as 1765. The Forecast function assumes a linear trend.

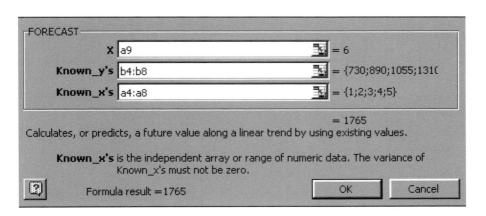

FIGURE 9.4

3 We will now use the Trend function to calculate how fast the cost of book advertising will continue to rise. We can use AutoFill to calculate it quickly rather than use Paste Function.
Select cell range **D4** to **D8** and move the mouse pointer onto the AutoFill

handle – this is the small square in the bottom right hand corner of the selected cell range.

Use the *right* mouse button to drag down – see Figure 9.5 – the linear trend figures are shown for each cell 'dragged'.

FIGURE 9.5

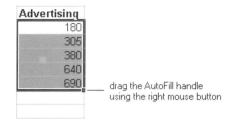

drag the AutoFill handle
using the right mouse button

Release the mouse button. Select either **LINEAR TREND** or **GROWTH TREND** from the pop up menu. You can use **EDIT-UNDO** to undo the trend calculation if necessary.

Note: You can also forecast by adding trendlines to charts – see Topic 4.

Further Functions

As mentioned at the beginning of this topic we cannot cover more than a fraction of the 200+ functions available in Excel. This section attempts to redress this by listing some further useful functions you have either used or might like to try:

(a) Date and time functions display dates and times, or can calculate the time elapsed between two dates or times; eg the function **NOW()** used in the first task of this topic.

(b) Financial functions calculate such things as investments, repayments and depreciation, eg:
   FV – calculates the future value function of an investment – see above.
   NPV – net present value of an investment.
   PMT calculates the repayments required on a loan – see above.
   SLN calculates depreciation using the straight-line method – see above.

(c) Statistical Functions – we have already used some of these in the second task of this unit **AVERAGE, MIN, MAX** and **STDEV.**

(d) Database Functions – we have already used some in Topic 5, eg **DAVERAGE, DMIN, DMAX, DSTDEV** and **DSUM**.

(e) Logical Functions test for the truth of certain conditions and include **IF, AND** and **OR**. We have used IF in the first task of this topic.

(f) The Lookup function **VLOOKUP** was used in Topic 7.

(g) Text Functions manipulate strings of text, eg **REPLACE, TRIM** and **UPPER**.

(h) Information Functions test cell references and contents, eg **TYPE, ISBLANK** and **ISERROR**.

TOPIC 10

Workbook Protection and Auditing

Introduction

This topic covers two main areas; protecting your workbook from deletion or alteration and ensuring that the the data entered is valid. The first task examines different levels of password protection and checks worksheet data for errors, the second task creates various types of data validation checks.

Topic Objectives

- To protect workbooks, worksheets and cell ranges.
- To check formulae for errors.
- To highlight changes in shared workbooks.
- To validate workbook data.

Workbook Protection

In Excel you can protect a workbook in various ways. The most secure form of protection is to prevent a workbook or a worksheet from being opened; appropriate for confidential information. You can also prevent others changing or deleting data or formulae in your workbook, ie read-only protection. Similar security is available for other workbook elements, eg charts or cell ranges.

 Workbook Protection. We will use the workbook **Summary2** in the folder **Car Hire** as it contains profit forecasts that could be confidential; however any workbook will do.

If a message appears, 'The workbook you opened contains automatic links.....' then click **YES**.

Select the **FILE-SAVE** as option and click the **TOOLS** button in the top right of the dialog box.

Select **GENERAL OPTIONS**. Various security options are offered – select the following:

Always Create Backup: Leave blank, if you select it then Excel creates a backup of the previous version of the workbook every time you save it.

Password to Open: Enter *jmuir* as the password. Take care entering it as the password is hidden behind a row of asterisks. The document cannot now be opened without this password.

Note: A password can consist of numbers, letters, spaces or symbols, up to 15 characters long – they are case sensitive. These levels of protection are not available for individual worksheets, only for the whole workbook.

Password to Modify: Enter *jmuir* again. This password prevents anyone from making any changes to the document. Someone opening the workbook who did not know the password would need to save the changed workbook under another name as a separate document.

Read-Only Recommended: Leave blank – this is the weakest form of protection: users are prompted, but not compelled, to open the workbook as read-only. This is useful to alert users not to make unnecessary changes.

Click **OK** and you are prompted to re-confirm both passwords – do so and the dialog box closes.

Click the **SAVE** button. As you have added password protection you will be asked if you wish to replace the original workbook – click **YES**.

2 Close the workbook **Summary2** and open it again. You will be asked for the passwords - enter them.
Make a small change to the workbook – you can do this as you know the password.

Note: to remove or change a password open the workbook and use the **FILE-SAVE AS-OPTIONS** as before.

3 Close the workbook.

4 **Worksheet Protection**. We will use the workspace file **Branch Profits**, in the folder **Car Hire,** but any workbook will do. If a message appears, 'The workbook you opened contains automatic links.....' click **YES**.
4 linked workbooks open – **Summary1** summarises 3 other workbooks using external references and formulae – these should be protected from alteration.
Maximise **Summary1** and select **FORMAT**-**CELLS** then the **PROTECTION** tab.
Select the **LOCKED** option if necessary (do not select the option **HIDDEN** which hides the formulae).
Click **OK**.

5 **Sheet Protection.** Select **TOOLS-PROTECTION-PROTECT SHEET**.
Select the **CONTENTS** option if necessary; it protects all cells in the sheet from amendment (de-select the Objects and Scenarios options as they do not apply to worksheets such as **Summary1**).
We won't use a password this time. Click **OK**.
If you now try to alter a cell in the **Summary1** workbook a dialog box warns you that it is locked.
Note: To unprotect a worksheet select **TOOLS-PROTECTION** then **UNPROTECT SHEET**.

6 **Protecting Individual Cells.** Sometimes only certain cells in the worksheet need protecting, not the whole sheet.
Maximise the workbook **Gatley**. Cells **B4** to **D7** contain data – these can be changed. The remaining cells contain formulae that should not be changed except by qualified staff. It is all too easy to destroy a complex worksheet by keying data into a cell containing crucial formulae.
Select cell range **B4** to **D7** first; these are the cells to remain unprotected.
Select **FORMAT-CELLS** and select the **PROTECTION** tab.

De-select the **LOCKED** option and click **OK**.

(7) Now protect the whole worksheet as in section 5 above using the **TOOLS-PROTECTION-PROTECT SHEET** as before.
Try and amend one of the cells in the range **B4** to **D7** – as they are now unprotected it should be possible. Use **EDIT- UNDO** to restore the original values.
If you try to alter a cell that contains a formula a dialog box warns you that it is locked.
Note: To unprotect a sheet use the options **TOOLS-PROTECTION-UNPROTECT** Sheet

(8) Protect the workbooks **Hale** and **Bowdon** in a similar way.

(9) **Protecting a Workbook.** So far we have protected workbooks or worksheets from being changed or opened. We can also prevent any new worksheets being added to a workbook and existing worksheets from being deleted or amended.
We will use the workbook **Bowdon** in the folder **Car Hire,** but any workbook will do. If a message appears, 'The workbook you opened contains automatic links.....' click **YES**.
Select **TOOLS-PROTECTION-PROTECT WORKBOOK**. Complete the dialog box as follows:
We won't use a password this time so leave it blank.
Select the **STRUCTURE** box if necessary; it protects the sheets in the workbook from being deleted, hidden, moved, or re-named.
Select the **WINDOWS** box if necessary; this prevents windows from being moved or re-sized. Click **OK**.

(10) Various options are now unavailable – check on the **EDIT** menu that **DELETE SHEET** and the **MOVE OR COPY SHEET** options are unavailable.
Check that the **INSERT-WORKSHEET** option is unavailable too.
Excel features allowing you to change the windows size are also hidden, eg the Minimise and Maximise buttons.

(11) Finally select **TOOLS-PROTECTION-UNPROTECT WORKBOOK** option to unprotect the workbook.

(12) Close all open workbooks – if you want to keep the protection then save them too.

Auditing Worksheet Data

'Real-life' worksheets can be extremely complex, occupying hundreds or thousands of cells and employing involved formulae and modelling; in these situations it is all too common for mistakes to creep in and invalidate the data. To help prevent this Excel provides a number of tools, some of which we have already used:

Naming Cells – using meaningful names for cells and cell ranges helps to make them easier to remember and to refer to rather than using cell references – see Topic 7.

Workbook Protection – stops unauthorised users from opening, changing or deleting data – see Task 1 above.

Document Overview – the Print Preview option and the Zoom button let you see more of the worksheet.

This task uses the Auditing Toolbar to trace back errors in related formulae and data.

1 **The Auditing Toolbar.** Open the workbook **Forecast Template** in the **Car Hire** folder.
Select **TOOLS-AUDITING-SHOW AUDITING TOOLBAR**.
Figure 10.1 shows a key to the Auditing Toolbar. Drag it to a new position if you need to so you can see the worksheet cells.

FIGURE 10.1

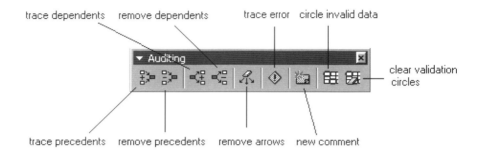

2 Select cell **D12** in the worksheet. Click the **TRACE PRECEDENTS** button; arrows trace the precedents for this cell, ie the cells on which the formula in cell D12 is built.
Try this for cell **E12** too.
Click the **REMOVE ALL ARROWS** button.

3 Now use the **TRACE DEPENDENTS** button to find the dependents for cells **B8** and **B10**, ie the chain of cells which directly and indirectly depend on them.
Remove the arrows as before.

4 **Tracing Errors:** Select cell **B5** and enter the letter **A**. The worksheet displays value errors as an arithmetic formula cannot use non-numeric characters.
Select cell **E12** then the **TRACE ERROR** button – the source of the error is shown.
Restore the value of cell B5 to 30 again to remove the errors.

5 Remove all the arrows and close the Auditing Toolbar.

6 **Viewing Formulae**. At a simpler level you can check which cells contain formulae and show the formulae.
Select **TOOLS-OPTIONS** then the **VIEW** tab.
Click the **FORMULAS** button in the **WINDOW OPTIONS** section.
All formulae are displayed and could be be checked and/or printed. Repeat these commands to de-select this option – the worksheet is restored to its normal appearance.

7 **Change Highlighting**. If you share the use of a workbook with co-workers, eg on a network, you can track the changes that have been made. To do this you have to enable two features – workbook sharing and change history. We will do this for demonstration purposes, however shared workbooks are limited in the Excel features that they can use – consult Excel Help before using this feature on a regular basis.

8 Select **TOOLS-TRACK CHANGES-HIGHLIGHT CHANGES**. Select the **TRACK CHANGES WHILE EDITING** box and the **HIGHLIGHT CHANGES ON SCREEN** options if necessary, and click **OK**. Save the workbook if prompted.

9 Make some amendments to the worksheet – to alert you to them Excel outlines the cells. When the mouse pointer is over a changed cell the change is described in a comment box.
Notes: the highlighting will also show if the worksheet is printed.
To turn off change highlighting, repeat step 8 to de-select the **TRACK CHANGES WHILE EDITING** option. The workbook is now no longer shared.

10 Close the **Forecast Template** workbook without saving it.

Data Validation in Worksheets

Data validation is a dominant concern in computer systems – how to ensure that users enter data correctly. Figure 10.2 is a summary of customer invoices; the following validation checks could be made when data is entered.

	A	B	C	D	E
1	Invoice Ref	Invoice Date	Customer No.	Customer Name	Invoice Value
2	A5418	08-Jun-00	2134	Singh Developments	658.00
3	A5419	05-Mar-00	1579	Berger Products	1437.00
4	A5420	31-Jan-00	2111	Webb Joinery	654.87
5	A5421	31-Jan-00	1093	Singh Electrical	2349.00
6	A5422	12-Apr-00	2198	Wilson's Golf	138.65
7	A5423	13-Apr-00	1532	Harris Publishing	2568.12
8	A5424	09-May-00	1579	Berger Products	188.00
9	A5425	09-May-00	2134	Singh Developments	19.91
10	A5426	20-Feb-00	1579	Berger Products	789.00
11	A5427	08-Mar-00	1478	Hamilton Media	905.99

FIGURE 10.2

Mandatory Entry: All items of information must be entered, no cells can be left blank.

Range/Limit Checks: Invoice values must fall within certain upper and lower limits.

Format Check: Most items entered should conform to a certain pattern of characters, eg all numeric, alphanumeric, date format.

Restrict data entered to options on a list, eg of approved customers.

1 Open the workbook **Databases** and copy the worksheet **Customer Invoices** using the **CTRL** key and drag and drop techniques. Rename it **Customer Invoices2**.
Select cell **C12** in **Customer Invoices2**.

2 When a new customer number is entered we might, eg, want it to be a 4 digit number in the range 2000 to 3000.
Select **DATA-VALIDATION** then the **SETTINGS** tab.
Make the following entries, using Figure 10.3 as a guide:

FIGURE 10.3

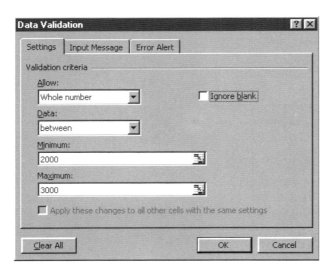

In the **ALLOW**: box select **WHOLE NUMBER.**
In the **DATA:** box select **BETWEEN**.
Enter the **Minimum** and **Maximum** quantities as in Figure 10.3.
De-select the **IGNORE BLANK** box.

3 We can also give the user instructions in entering the data, select the **INPUT MESSAGE** tab and complete it as shown in Figure 10.4.

FIGURE 10.4

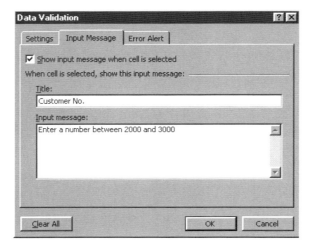

4 When cell **C12** is selected an instruction box is displayed to guide you. If you enter an invalid number outside the range a standard error message appears – try this.

5 We can create our own error message. Make sure that cell C12 is still selected and select **DATA-VALIDATION** then the **ERROR ALERT** tab. Try out different messages and styles.
Enter an invalid number again and this time a customised warning message appears.

6 **Independent Tasks.**
Validate the Invoice date cell B12 to restrict dates to the year 2000.
Validate the Invoice Ref cell A12 to a text length of 5.

7 **Validation Checks-Copying.** Once you have created validation checks for one cell and checked that they are working correctly you can copy them to other relevant cells.
Select cell **C12**, containing the customer number validation.
Select **EDIT-COPY**.
Select the other customer number cells, ie **C2** to **C11**.
Select **EDIT-PASTE SPECIAL**.
Click the **VALIDATION** button in the dialog box then **OK**.
Now try out the validation for these cells.

8 **Highlighting Invalid Data**. Select the options **TOOLS-AUDITING-SHOW AUDITING TOOLBAR**.
Click the **CIRCLE INVALID DATA** button on the Auditing toolbar; cells not in the range 2000 to 3000 are circled – see section 2 above.
Note: The circles can be removed using the **CLEAR VALIDATION CIRCLES** button on the Auditing Toolbar.

89

9 **Choosing Entries from a List**. It is possible to restrict entries to a list, eg of customer names. Normally we would create the list in a separate cell range, but as an example we will use the existing customer names.
Select cell **D12** and then the menu options **DATA-VALIDATION**. On the **SETTINGS** tab choose **LIST** from the **ALLOW** box.
Enter the formula **=D2:D11** in the **SOURCE** box; these are the cells that hold the customer names.
De-select the **IGNORE BLANK** box – this will ensure that the customer name cannot be left blank.
Click **OK**; the down arrow button on the cell means that the user can only select the customer names in the list. There would normally be no duplicate names in such a list.

Notes: A validation check can be removed by calling up the dialog box as before and selecting 'any value'.
To make sure that the user inputs a number but not within any particular range specify a number not equal to 0.

Macros

Introduction

This topic introduces Excel macros. At its simplest a macro lets you record and save a series of keyboard strokes, menu choices and mouse movements and run them again whenever you need to. This has the advantage of saving time – issuing the same series of commands manually is time consuming. A macro can also achieve greater consistency and accuracy by reducing the need for users to enter long sequences of commands. More generally the creators of macros can control the user interface, they can, eg, disable standard menus and screen features and add ones of their own, including user instructions, error messages, custom menus and dialog boxes. Systems developers can in effect design a complete customised system. This is especially important when users of varying skill and knowledge are using a worksheet and could damage it by deleting or altering vital data. Excel 2000 uses the Visual Basic for Applications programming language (VBA) version 6, specially developed for Microsoft Office macros and applications. Macros are stored in special module sheets and can control charts and databases as well as worksheets. In this topic we shall be starting with some simple macros which automate straightforward tasks. In the next topic we shall be building a small user application using macros.

Topic Objectives

- To record a macro.
- To assign a macro to a shortcut key.
- To assign a macro to a button.
- To run a macro automatically.
- To run and test macros.
- To appreciate problems caused by macro viruses.
- To view the module sheet holding the VBA code.
- To use macros to print and format worksheets.

More Information on Macros

Every macro is saved and run under a different name. The macro name can be up to 255 characters long, must begin with a letter, and can include letters, numbers, full stops or underscores. As spaces are not allowed in macro names underscores or full stops are often used instead. Macro names are not case sensitive. A macro can be run in several ways, the easiest way is to assign the macro its own special button or menu option. It can also be run using a keyboard shortcut – a combination of the Ctrl key and a single letter. The letter that you use *is* case-sensitive however, eg Ctrl -e would run a particular macro; Ctrl-E would not. Although in theory therefore you have 52 shortcut key combinations, many are already existing Excel keyboard shortcuts, eg

Ctrl-S to save. If you used this combination to run a macro then the normal keyboard shortcut would not work in the workbook that contains the macro, so existing shortcut keys are best avoided.

A Simple Date-Stamp Macro

For a simple macro you can use the macro recorder which records such actions as mouse movements, menu selections and keystrokes. The recorded macro can be 'played back' any time it is required. Instead of keying in the NOW() function into a cell to show the current system date and time we will record the key strokes etc involved and assign them the keyboard shortcut Ctrl-e (letters a-d are already used as Excel keyboard commands).

1 Open the Workbook **Discount**. Any workbook will do if you don't have this workbook, but you may need to change some cell references.
Select **TOOLS-MACRO-RECORD NEW MACRO**. Use Figure 11.1. as a guide to completing the Record Macro dialog box.

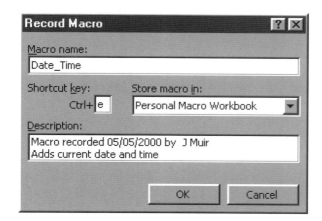

FIGURE 11.1

2 Enter the macro name as **Date_Time**.
Enter the letter **e** in the **CTRL+** box.

3 Click the down arrow on the **STORE MACRO IN:** box and select the option **PERSONAL MACRO WORKBOOK**.

Note: There are three locations where you can store macros.

(a) The **Personal** macro workbook is a special workbook that opens automatically whenever you start Excel. You can use it to store and run macros that will apply to more than one workbook.

(b) The 'This Workbook' option stores macros on a module sheet in the current workbook. This is useful when the macro will only apply to this workbook.

(c) 'New Workbook' stores the macro in a new workbook. We will not use this option as you would have to open the workbook in order to run the macro.

4 Select the **DESCRIPTION** box and add a description of the macro, eg *'Adds Current Date & Time'*. The creation date and the name of the author or organisation are added automatically.
Click the **OK** button and a 'Recording' message is displayed at the bottom left of the screen; the Stop Recording toolbar displays with a Stop Macro button.

5 **Macro Recording.** The macro recorder is now waiting for you to record the macro steps. As any action will be recorded it is important not to make any unnecessary mouse movements, keystrokes or menu selections etc.

(a) Select cell **A1.**

(b) Type the function **=NOW()** in cell **A1** then click the 'tick' button or press `ENTER`.

(c) Select the menu options **FORMAT-CELLS-NUMBER**.

(d) Select the **DATE** category, and select a suitable date/time format.

(e) Click **OK** and the date is displayed in cell A1. If the column displays a row of '####' symbols then the column needs to be widened to display the date.

(f) Click the **STOP RECORDING** button (if you can't see it select **TOOLS-MACRO-STOP RECORDING**).

(g) Check the Recording message is no longer displayed. Now that we have recorded the Date_Time macro let's see where it has been stored.

6 **How Macros are Stored.** We have stored this macro in the Personal macro workbook which is normally hidden. Select the options **WINDOW-UNHIDE** and then **PERSONAL** to show it.
Select **TOOLS-MACRO-MACROS**. The Macro dialog box lists all the macros associated with a workbook; at present we have only created one – Date_Time.
Click **EDIT** to show the module sheet. This is where the macro is stored as a very simple Visual Basic (VBA) program; it consists of a single subroutine or 'Sub' – Date_Time(). Apart from introductory comments, shown in green, it contains three VBA commands:
Range("A1")Select
ActiveCell.FormulaR1C1 = "now()"
Selection.NumberFormat = "d/m/yy h.mm am/pm"
If the date format is incorrect you can edit it directly on the macro sheet.
Click the topmost **CLOSE** button to return to the worksheet.
Select **WINDOW-HIDE** to hide the Personal workbook.

7 *Note*: **If your Macro was Wrongly Recorded**. As the Macro Recorder records all your actions, correct or incorrect, you may sometimes press the wrong key or make the wrong menu selection. If so it is best to stop recording, delete the incorrect macro and try again. Select **TOOLS-MACRO-MACROS**, then select the macro from the dialog box and click the Delete option. If the macro is in the Personal workbook then you must un-hide it first to do this – see previous section.

8 **Running the Date-Time Macro**. Simply hold down the `CTRL` key then press the e key – the macro will run and update the time. As the macro is stored in the Personal workbook it will only work while this workbook is open. Wait for two minutes and try the following:

(a) **Unhide** the Personal workbook again and then close and save it.

(b) Now try running the macro as before using `CTRL-e`. This time nothing will happen, ie the time will not be updated as the special Personal workbook has been closed.

(c) Open the Personal workbook – you may need to use the Find tool on the Open dialog box to locate it – use the **TOOLS** button. Before you can open it you have to respond to a virus warning – see below.

(9) **Macro Viruses.** When you open any workbook containing macros, such as the Personal workbook, Excel will alert you to the danger of hidden viruses. The dialog box has 3 option buttons, click 'More Info' for Help text. Macro viruses have become one of the most common virus types and are activated whenever an infected workbook is opened. A macro virus can also be spread if the workbook is opened via a network (including the Web). All that Excel does is to detect the presence of macros in a workbook and display this warning message before it opens. To detect and remove any viruses that may be present you would need to have antivirus software installed. Close the Help text and return to the warning dialog box; the two other options are:

Enable Macros: This option will open the workbook and enable the macros. If the workbook comes from a known, reliable source then this is OK. Often a workbook will not work properly without the macros enabled so the temptation is to take this option, however, if the workbook is from an unfamiliar source, especially the Internet, and you did not expect it to contain macros, then it is safest either to use a virus checker first or to take the next option –

Disable Macros: This will open the workbook with the macros disabled – a safer option which will allow you to view and edit macros but not run them. Bear in mind, however, that the macro-driven features will not work.

(10) Click **ENABLE MACROS** and then hide the Personal workbook as before. Now try running the macro as before using `CTRL-e`. This time it will run.

(11) Leave the **Discount** workbook open and open the workbook **Loan Table**. Any workbook will do if you don't have this workbook, but you may need to change some cell references.
Run the macro again and the date and time will be added to cell A1 of the **Loan Table** workbook. As the macro is held in the Personal workbook it will work for any workbook.
Close the workbook **Loan Table** but keep the workbook **Discount** open.

(12) **Running a Macro from the Tools Menu**. You can run a macro for test purposes from the Tools menu – select **TOOLS-MACRO-MACROS**.
In the dialog box select, eg, the Date_Time macro and click **RUN**.

(13) **Review – Recording a Macro.** (Information only)

(a) Select **TOOLS-MACRO-RECORD NEW MACRO**.

(b) Enter the macro name, description, any shortcut letter and the workbook where the macro will be held in the Record Macro dialog box.

(c)   Record the steps of the macro.

(d)   Click the Stop Macro button (or select **TOOLS-MACRO-STOP RECORDING**).

Running a Macro from a Button

We have learnt how to run a macro using a shortcut key and to run it from the Macro menu. You can also run a macro by clicking a button; the button can be placed either on the worksheet or on a toolbar. We will create a button that runs a special print macro.

1   Open the workbook **Loan Table**. Any workbook will do if you don't have this workbook, but you may need to change some cell references.
The loan interest table in cell range A7 to C17 can be printed using a print macro.

2   Select **VIEW-TOOLBARS** and select the **FORMS** toolbar. Click the Button tool – see Figure 11.2 – and the screen pointer changes to cross hairs.

FIGURE 11.2

3   **Drawing the Button.** Drag to create a button covering cells **E2** and **E3**. A button is displayed with the default name '**BUTTON1**'; it can be moved and re-sized later if necessary.

4   **Linking the Button with a Macro.** The Assign Macro dialog box appears now.

(a)   First close the **FORMS** toolbar then click the **RECORD** button on the Assign Macro dialog box.

(b)   The **RECORD MACRO** dialog box is displayed next; complete it as follows:

(c)   Name the macro **Print_Loan_Table**.

(d)   Do not enter anything in the **SHORTCUT KEY** box as the macro will be run from a button.

(e)   In the **STORE MACRO IN** box select the option **THIS WORKBOOK**. The loan table is in a cell range that only applies to this workbook so there is no point in storing the macro in the Personal macro workbook.

(f) Enter a description of the macro in the Description box, eg, *'Prints the loan interest table'*.

(g) Click **OK** – you have assigned the macro to a button and you can now record it.

5 **Macro Recording.** Proceed as follows:

(a) Check the printer is turned on.

(b) Select the options **FILE-PAGE SETUP** and select the **SHEET** tab.

(c) In the **PRINT AREA** box enter the cell range **A7:C17**.

(d) Click **OK**.

(e) Select the option **FILE-PRINT**; choose options such as number of copies.

(f) Click **OK**.

(g) The loan table will print; when printing is finished click the **STOP RECORDING** button (if you can't see it select **TOOLS-MACRO-STOP RECORDING**).
     The print macro is now created as part of the Loan Table workbook.

(h) **Troubleshooting** – see section 11 below.

6 **Button Formatting – Font.** The button that we created earlier can be formatted, providing it is correctly selected first, ie press the **CTRL** key and then click the button – it will be enclosed in 'selection' handles (if you merely click the button this will run the macro and print off the table again).
     Delete the default name then select the menu options **FORMAT-CONTROL** and choose font size **8** from the **SIZE** box.
     Use the down arrow button on the **COLOUR** box to choose a colour for the button text.
     Click **OK** - the button should be still selected; type the new label for the button, eg *'Click to Print'*.
     To de-select the button click elsewhere on the worksheet or press the **ESC** key.

7 *Note:* **Button Size and Position.** Select the button as before and drag one of the selection handles to change its size – the screen pointer is now a double-headed arrow shape.
     To move the button place the screen pointer on the edge of the button – not on a selection handle – and drag. If you move the button within the print area the button will be printed too.

8 **Running the Macro.** To run the macro simply click the button and the cell range should be printed as before – see section 11 for troubleshooting.

9 **Viewing the Macro:** The macro is stored in the workbook it controls – the Loan Table workbook. Select the options **TOOLS-MACRO-MACROS**, then select the **Print_Loan_Table** macro and click **EDIT**.

Maximise the module sheet to display the macro. The VBA code is much longer than the first macro as it includes the standard page setup settings.

Click the topmost **CLOSE** button to return to the worksheet.

(10) Save and close the workbook.

(11) **Troubleshooting – Information only:** As the Macro Recorder records all your actions, correct or incorrect, you may find that the Print_Loan_Table macro does not work as it should. If so delete it and try again. Select **TOOLS-MACRO-MACROS**, then select the macro from the dialog box and click the **DELETE** option. To delete a button simply select the button as before (**CTRL- CLICK**) and press the **DELETE** key.

Consolidation

A print macro such as the Print_Loan_Table macro sets a print area that will probably only apply to one worksheet and workbook. This task gives you more practice in creating a print macro for another workbook

(1) Open the workbook **Domestic Help** (or any other suitable workbook) and create a new macro to print off the list of helpers.

(2) Name the macro **Print_Helpers** and assign it a shortcut key.

(3) Create a print button for the macro too.

(4) Test both shortcut key and button.

Running a Macro from a Toolbar Button

This task will assign a macro to a button on a toolbar. You can use either an existing button or your own custom button. We will use a custom button which will run a macro to format a worksheet. We will select the custom button, add it to the Formatting Toolbar, assign a macro to it and then record it.

(1) Open the workbook **Insurance Sales**. Drag aside any embedded chart so that you can see the worksheet data. Any workbook will do if you don't have this workbook, but you may need to change some cell references.

(2) **Selecting the Custom Button.**

(a) Select **TOOLS-CUSTOMISE** then the **COMMANDS** tab.

(b) Select **MACROS** from the **CATEGORIES** list – scroll down if necessary.

(c) Use the screen pointer to drag the custom button *from* the dialog box *onto* the **FORMATTING** Toolbar next to the **BOLD** button – see Figure 11.3. Do *not* close the Customise dialog box.

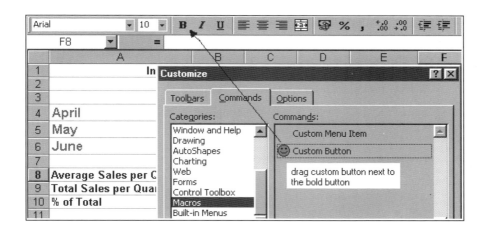

FIGURE 11.3

3 **Choosing a Custom Button Design**.

(a) Right click the custom button *on the toolbar* (not in the dialog box).

(b) Select the **CHANGE BUTTON IMAGE** option.

(c) Select another button icon.

(d) Close the Customise dialog box.

4 **Recording the Customise Macro**.

(a) Select the options **TOOLS-MACRO-RECORD NEW MACRO**.

(b) In the dialog box enter the macro name **Format_Worksheet**.

(c) Do not enter anything in the **SHORTCUT KEY** box as the macro will be run from the custom button.

(d) In the **STORE MACRO in** box select the option **THIS WORKBOOK**. The formatting will only apply to this workbook so there is no point in storing the macro in the Personal macro workbook.

(e) Enter a description of the macro in the Description box, eg, *'Formats the worksheet'*.

(f) Click **OK** – you have assigned the macro to a button and you can now record it.

5 Select the cell range holding the insurance data – **A1** to **E10**.
Select the options **FORMAT-AUTOFORMAT** and choose the format **COLORFUL** 2.
Click **OK**.
Click the **STOP MACRO** button (if the button is not visible then use the menu options **TOOLS-MACRO-STOP RECORDING**).

6 **Assigning the Macro**. Click the custom button on the toolbar.
Select the macro **FORMAT_WORKSHEET** from the macro dialog box.

7 **Testing the Formatting Macro**. First remove the autoformatting and restore the worksheet to its normal format. With the cell range still selected select **FORMAT-AUTOFORMAT** again and select the format **NONE** and click **OK**.

Now click the custom button and the macro should reformat the worksheet cells to the AutoFormat previously recorded.

(8) **Viewing the Macro:** The macro is stored in the workbook it controls – the Insurance Sales workbook. Select the options **TOOLS-MACRO-MACROS**, then select the **FORMAT_WORKSHEET** macro and click **EDIT**.
Maximise the Module sheet to display the macro.
Click the topmost **CLOSE** button to return to the worksheet.

(9) **Troubleshooting – Information only:**

(a) As the Macro Recorder records all your actions, correct or incorrect, you may find that the formatting macro does not work as it should. If so delete it and try again. Select **TOOLS-MACRO-MACROS**, select the macro from the dialog box and click the Delete option.

(b) **Deleting a Custom Toolbar Button.** Select the options **TOOLS-CUSTOMISE** and select the **COMMANDS** tab.
Select **MACROS** from the **CATEGORIES** list and drag the custom button *from* the toolbar back *to* the dialog box.

(10) Close the Insurance Sales workbook. Save it if you wish to keep the formatting macro.

Macros That Run Automatically

(1) Sometimes we wish to run a macro automatically every time the workbook is opened. We will automatically run the Date_Time macro so that when a workbook is opened it enters the current date and time. Open the workbook **Discount**. If you get a virus warning click 'Enable Macros'.

(2) Select the options **INSERT-NAME-DEFINE**. Select the **NAMES IN WORKBOOK** box and enter the name **Auto_Open** (a name used to call macros automatically when a workbook is opened must begin with the words Auto_Open).

(3) Select the **REFERS TO** box next and type **=Personal.xls!Date_Time** this box now contains the name of the macro that is being called – the Date-Time macro, created in Task 1. As this macro is stored in another workbook – Personal – the name of this workbook must be included too.
Click **OK**.

(4) To test the macro delete any date and time from cell A1 then save and close the workbook.

(5) Open the workbook **Discount** again. If you get a virus warning click 'Enable Macros'.
The Date_Time macro should be run automatically and the date and time inserted.

(6) **Troubleshooting.** If you get an error message then make the following checks:

(a) Select **INSERT-NAME-DEFINE** again and select the name **AUTO_OPEN**.

(b) Check the spelling and syntax of the entry in the name box - there must be no spaces and you must use the underscore (_) not the dash.

(c) Check the spelling of the macro in the **REFERS TO:** box.

(d) To test the macro save and close the workbook and open it again.

    Notes: To run a macro automatically when you close a workbook proceed as above but use a name that begins with **Auto_Close**.
If you want to run more than one macro automatically from the same workbook use several names, each beginning with **Auto_Close** or **Auto_Open**.

TOPIC 12

Creating a Custom Application

Introduction

This topic covers the creation of an invoicing template where you can enter customer and order line details. Details of the invoice are then automatically transferred to a database, using Excel's Template Wizard. We will also create a special user menu to automate certain of the invoicing tasks.

Topic Objectives

- To design the layout of an online form.
- To incorporate Clip Art and Word Art effects in a form.
- To protect areas of a form from amendment.
- To create a database using Template Wizard.
- To design a custom menu.
- To assign macros to menu options.

Designing The Form Heading

1 Open a new workbook. Select **FORMAT-COLUMN-STANDARD WIDTH**. Set the width to 7.

FIGURE 12.1

2 The heading section of the invoice form will contain the company logo, address and other details – see Figure 12.1. Make sure that Drawing Toolbar is displayed at the bottom of screen, if not select **VIEW-TOOLBARS**.

3 Select the range of cells **A1** to **K6** and click the **MERGE AND CENTRE** button on the Formatting Toolbar, it is marked with a small 'a' between two arrows. The cell area selected is blank, becoming in effect one large cell.

4 To insert the wine bottle logo proceed as follows:

(a) Click the **INSERT CLIP ART** button on the Drawing Toolbar, then select the **PICTURES** tab.

(b) Select **ENTERTAINMENT** from the list of categories. Right click the wine bottle image and select **COPY**.

(c) Close the Insert Clip Art dialog box. You are returned to the worksheet; select **EDIT-PASTE**. The picture is inserted but at the moment it is too large. Close the Picture Toolbar if necessary.

(d) Right click the image and choose **FORMAT PICTURE**; on the dialog box that appears click the **SIZE** tab and adjust the size to about 5 cms high and 3cms wide.

(e) Drag and re-size so the image covers cells **A1** to **B6** – see Figure 12.1.

5 Now click the **WORD ART** button on the Drawing Toolbar. Select a suitable style and click **OK**.
Type the company name *Quality Wines* in the dialog box that appears next and click **OK**. Drag and re-size so the image covers cells **C1** to **G6** – see Figure 12.1.

6 Now use the Text Box tool to draw a text box covering cells **H1** to **K6** and enter some address details – see Figure 12.1. You can change the text size and style in the usual ways.

7 Finally we will mark off the heading section with a line. Select cell range **A7** to **K7**. Select the options **FORMAT-CELLS-BORDER**. Select a thick line that will form a border along the *top* of these cells – see Figure 2.3 if necessary.

101

Designing the Customer Information Section

1 This section will hold details of the customer; it will consist of a series of labelled data entry boxes for name, address etc - see Figure 12.2.

2 Adjust the height of row 8 to about 20.00 by dragging the row divider downwards.
Enter the text label *'Customer Invoice No:'* in cell **B8** and create a border around cells **E8** to **F8** as shown in Figure 12.2.

3 Repeat these steps for the labelled data entry box 'Invoice date'.

4 Now, using Figure 12.2 as a guide, create a series of merged cells as follows to hold the customer information labels:

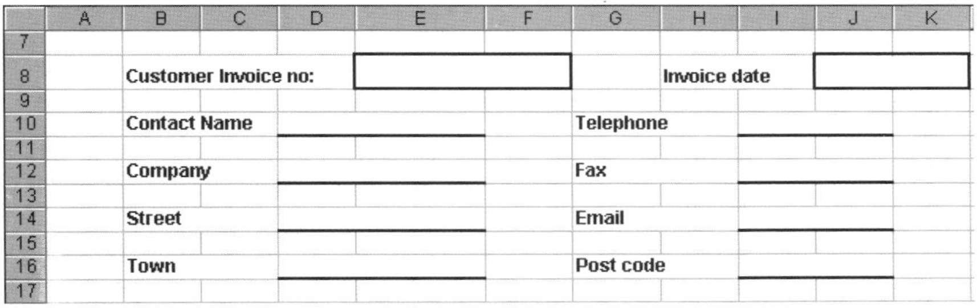

FIGURE 12.2

Merge cells **B10** and **C10**. Enter the label *'Contact Name'* in bold.
Merge cells **B12** and **C12**. Enter the label *'Company'* in bold.
Merge cells **B14** and **C14**. Enter the label *'Street'* in bold.
Merge cells **B16** and **C16**. Enter the label *'Town'* in bold.
Merge cells **G10** and **H10**. Enter the label *'Telephone'* in bold.
Merge cells **G12** and **H12**. Enter the label *'Fax'* in bold.
Merge cells **G14** and **H14**. Enter the label *'Email'* in bold.
Merge cells **G16** and **H16**. Enter the label *'Post code'* in bold.

(5) *Note*: if you want to split a merged cell back into separate cells then select the cell and open the Format menu and choose the Cells option then the Alignment tab. You can then de-select the 'Merge cells' checkbox.

(6) We now need to create merged, underlined cells to hold the customer data that will be entered. Start by selecting cells cells **D10** and **E10**. Merge them and then underline them using the **FORMAT-CELLS-BORDER** options. Repeat these actions to emphasise the data entry areas next to each label using Figure 12.2 as a guide.

(7) We have now completed the first two sections of the sales invoice. Open the **FILE** menu and select **PRINT PREVIEW** to check that it will print within the limits of an A4 page. If not then you will need to adjust column widths or page margins.

Designing the Invoice Information Section

(1) The next section will hold details of the items that the customer has purchased. The first part of it will be the title.
Select cell range **A18** to **K18** and merge it,
Enter the title *'Items Supplied'* as shown in Figure 12.3. Make the font size about 20 and centre and embolden it.

(2) The main part of the invoice information section will consist of a list of wines supplied to the customer. In rows 21 and 22 enter the 5 column headings shown in Figure 12.3: *Order Line, Stock Code, Stock Desc., Quantity Supplied, Unit Price (£)* and *Total Value*. `

(3) As this is a template invoice there is no need to enter details of wines; this will be done when an actual invoice is created. However, we can enter the formulae for the Total Value amounts shown in column H. These are produced by multiplying the quantity and the unit price amounts in columns F and G. Enter the first formula and then use the Edit menu to fill down. A series of zeros will appear in cells H23 to H32.

(4) *Note*: Avoid widening the columns too much as this may alter the alignment of previous sections of the invoice and make the invoice too wide to print on an A4 page – check this using print preview if necessary.

(5) Enter the three cell labels *Subtotal*, **VAT** and *Total* in cells **G34** to **G36** as shown in Figure 12.3.
Now select cell **H34** and calculate the subtotal of the 10 sales lines using a SUM function. If you have used the cells shown then the formula will be
=SUM(H23:H32)

	A	B	C	D	E	F	G	H
17								
18					**Items Supplied**			
19								
20								
21			Order	Stock	Stock	Quantity	Unit	Total
22			Line	Code	Desc		Price (£)	Value
23			1					0
24			2					0
25			3					0
26			4					0
27			5					0
28			6					0
29			7					0
30			8					0
31			9					0
32			10					0
33								
34							Subtotal	0
35							VAT	0
36							Total	0
37								

FIGURE 12.3

6. To calculate the current VAT rate of 17.5% involves multiplying the subtotal by 0.175, so the formula to be entered in cell H35 is **=H34*0.175**
Now add the values in cells **H34** and **H35** by using another SUM function in cell **H36**.

7. Now we will save the workbook as a template. Open the **FILE** menu and select **SAVE AS**. Name the workbook **Invoicing Application**. Click the down arrow on the **SAVE AS TYPE** box and select **TEMPLATE**. Excel will automatically select the Templates folder to store it in; this means that when you come to create a new invoice this template workbook will be listed on the General tab. Finally click **SAVE**.

8. Name the worksheet **Sales Invoice**.

9. **Optional Activities**.

(a) To improve the appearance of the template invoice further you could turn off the gridlines to emphasise the data entry areas. Open the **TOOLS** menu and select **OPTIONS**; you will see that the Gridlines options can be deleted.

(b) Another possibility is to shade or colour cells containing labels or data entry areas. You can get other ideas about style and presentation from the sample template applications provided by Excel; Open the **FILE** menu and select **NEW**, then click the **SPREADSHEET SOLUTIONS** tab. You will find that the Invoicing template has some good ideas about marking off the different section of the form.

Protecting the Worksheet

Now that the template invoice is nearly complete we need to protect its components from accidental alteration, in particular the heading section, the cell labels and the formulae. The parts of the invoice that the user will fill in need to remain amendable.

Note: When this template is copied to create an invoice the protected parts of the worksheet will still be protected in the copy.

① **Protecting Cells.** First we need to select the various areas of the worksheet that need to remain amendable. Start from the top of the invoice and, holding down the **CTRL** key, select the following cells (assuming that your worksheet layout uses the same cells as the ones used above):

(a) In rows **8** to **16** select the 10 merged cells next to the data labels that will hold the customer details.

(b) Select cell range **D23** to **G32**, holding details of the items supplied.

② Open the **FORMAT** menu and select the **CELLS** option – the **FORMAT CELLS** dialog box appears.
Click the **PROTECTION** tab and click the **LOCKED** option box to de-select it.
Finally click **OK**.

③ Now open the **TOOLS** menu and select the options **PROTECTION-PROTECT SHEET** to protect the whole worksheet.
Check that the cells selected and unlocked in section 1 above are unprotected by attempting to alter them. You will find that it is possible. Experiment if you wish, but restore the original values. Finally check that the remainder of the worksheet areas are protected from alteration. If you are happy with the protection save the changes.
Note: To unprotect a sheet open the **TOOLS** menu and select the options **PROTECTION** then **UNPROTECT SHEET**.

Creating a Database using Template Wizard

We have now created a template invoice which can be used to enter details of the customer and the items they have purchased. Every time a new invoice is to be issued the template workbook **Invoicing Application** is opened, the details filled in and the invoice saved under another name so that the original template is not overwritten. However, we also need to keep a separate record of all the invoices issued. This can be a simple list or table of, eg, the invoice date, invoice number, customer details, plus the total invoice value. Excel lets you create a database in a separate template workbook using Template Wizard.

① Open the **DATA** menu and select **TEMPLATE WIZARD** (if this option is not on the Data menu then it has not been installed and you will need to do so using the Excel Setup CDROM).

② The **STEP 1** dialog box appears, offering 2 edit boxes: the first holds the name of the workbook acting as the source for the template, the second is for the name of the new template workbook that will hold the database. To find out more about this click the **HELP** button on the dialog box.
Check that the first dialog box holds the name of the template workbook that we have just created – **Invoicing Application**, then click on the second edit box and use the right arrow key to check the name and path of

the new workbook. The path can be left as it is, as by default all templates are stored in a special Templates folder (part of the Microsoft Office or Excel folder). The name can also be the same as the source workbook – Excel automatically adds the word 'database' to the name. Click the **NEXT** button.

(3) The **STEP** 2 dialog box allows you to select the database type. Check that **MICROSOFT EXCEL WORKBOOK** is selected and that the name and location are correct. Click the **NEXT** button.

(4) **STEP** 3 lets you select the cell values and field names (ie the data labels) that will be transferred from the Invoicing Application template to the Invoicing Application Database. It is simply a matter of clicking the appropriate cell in the Invoicing Application workbook then the cell in the Template Wizard dialog box.
Using Figure 12.4 as a guide make the following selections:

(a) Make sure that cell 1 is selected on the Template Wizard dialog box.

(b) Click cell **E8** on the worksheet – the cell that holds the invoice number.

(c) Click this cell and its reference is transferred to cell 1 of the dialog box; it will appear as an absolute reference – **$E$8**.

(d) Now click the first Field Name cell on the dialog box and the field name *'Customer Invoice No.'* should automatically appear. If not you may have to enter it manually.

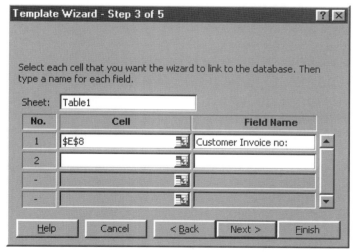

FIGURE 12.4

(5) Now repeat these steps for the following cells and field names: *Invoice date*, *Contact Name*, *Company*, *Street*, *Town* and *Total*. Eventually you should end up with 7.
Click the **NEXT** button.

(6) **STEP** 4 gives you the option of adding information from an existing workbook; as this is a new application select **NO** then the **NEXT** button.

(7) **STEP 5**, the final step, summarises where the template and the database will be stored – you may find that the complete path is not displayed – and

explains how the database can be shared; click the **FINISH** button.
Now save and close the template workbook **Invoicing Application**.

Using the Invoicing Template to Enter Data

1 Open the **FILE** menu and select **NEW**. Make sure that the **GENERAL** tab is selected.
You should see 2 icons listed, one labelled 'Invoicing Application' and the other 'Invoicing Application Database'. This is the database we have just created in the previous task; it will be used purely to hold data entered via the invoicing application. Open **Invoicing Application** again. Take the 'Enable Macros' option on the dialog box that appears.

2 Now test the template by entering some customer data, plus one or two order items.
Open the **FILE** menu and select **SAVE**. A dialog box apears, offering you 3 options; take the second one **CREATE A NEW RECORD**. This will write the invoice details to the database. Click **OK**.
The **SAVE AS** dialog box appears next; this appears because we don't want to save the invoice details to the Invoicing Application template as it should remain an empty framework, instead we want to save the details of the invoice to a new workbook.

3 Make sure that the **SAVE AS** type box is set to **MICROSOFT EXCEL WORKBOOK** and give the invoice a suitable name and folder. Click **SAVE** – the invoice details entered have now been saved in a new workbook. Close this workbook.

4 Open the **FILE** menu and select **NEW**. Make sure that the **GENERAL** tab is selected.
Open **INVOICING APPLICATION DATABASE** – it holds the new database created by Template Wizard, at the moment consisting of just 2 rows, the field headings and the invoice details. Make sure that the correct field names are displayed – adjust the column widths if necessary. Also check that the invoice details have been correctly transferred.

Note: Do not use this worksheet for any other purpose or it may not work correctly as a database.

Designing a Custom Menu

1 To finish off the invoicing application we will create a custom menu, offering the user the options of printing the invoice form, clearing the form or hiding the menu.
Open the workbook **Invoicing Application** again with macros enabled.
Select **TOOLS-CUSTOMIZE** and select the **TOOLBARS** tab.
Click the **NEW** button – use the New Toolbars dialog box to name the menu **Invoicing**.

Note: In Excel a custom menu is classed as a toolbar.

2 The new menu bar is displayed on the worksheet, adjacent to the Customize dialog box; at the moment it resembles a button – make sure that it remains over the main worksheet area during the following activities. If you check the list of toolbars in the Customize dialog box you will see that the new Invoicing toolbar is listed.

3 Click the **COMMANDS** tab and select **NEW MENU** from the **CATEGORIES** list.

Now use the mouse pointer to drag this option *from* the dialog box *onto* the Invoicing button – see Figure 12.5.

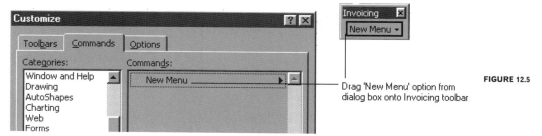

Drag 'New Menu' option from dialog box onto Invoicing toolbar

FIGURE 12.5

4 Click the **MODIFY SELECTION** button on the **CUSTOMIZE** dialog box and rename the first option **INVOICES** – the Invoicing button should now resemble Figure 12.6.

107

FIGURE 12.6

5 Click the down arrow on the **INVOICES** option on the **INVOICING** button – an empty drop down box appears – see Figure 12.7.

FIGURE 12.7

6 Now make sure that the **COMMANDS** tab is still selected in the **CUSTOMIZE** dialog box. This time select **MACRO** from the Categories list. Use the mouse pointer to drag the **CUSTOM MENU ITEM** option *from* the dialog box *onto* the drop down box; it should now resemble Figure 12.8, ie you should now have two menu items, the first, 'Invoices' will eventually be the menu title, the second 'Custom Menu Item' will be the first menu option.

FIGURE 12.8

7 Drag the **CUSTOM MENU ITEM** option again from the dialog box onto the bottom of the second item; repeat once more and your custom menu should look like Figure 12.9.

Note: To delete an unwanted menu item simply right click it and select **DELETE**.

FIGURE 12.9

8 We will now rename the 3 menu items at present called 'Custom Menu Item'. Right click each in turn and rename them respectively *'Print form'*, *Clear form'* and *'Hide invoicing menu'*.

9 We now need to attach the menu to a location in the workbook. Click the **TOOLBARS** tab and check that the Invoicing toolbar is selected. Click the **ATTACH** button on the Customize dialog box.
In the **ATTACH TOOLBARS** dialog box make sure that **INVOICING** is selected in the left hand section and click the **COPY** button – it is copied to the right hand section and attached to the Invoicing Application workbook when you click **OK**.

10 Now close the **CUSTOMIZE** dialog box and drag the custom menu (see note below) to the top of the workbook window – it is allocated its own menu space – see Figure 12.10.

Note: The custom menu, like all toolbars, can be moved to any part of the worksheet, using its special 'move' handle. Be very careful doing this when the Customize dialog box is open. If you accidentally 'drag' on another part of the custom menu it is very easy to delete menu options which will then need re-creating.

use 'move' handle to
drag menu

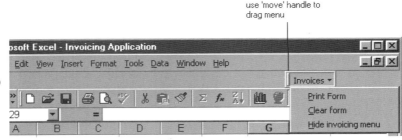

FIGURE 12.10

Macros to Control the Invoice Form

1   Now that the custom menu is created we need to create three macros and assign them to each of the three menu options. Our first, which will print the invoice form, is straightforward – we created a similar one in the previous topic.

(a) Select the options **TOOLS-MACRO-RECORD NEW MACRO**.

(b) The **RECORD MACRO** dialog box is displayed next; complete it as follows:

(c) Name the macro **Print_Invoice.**

(d) Do not enter anything in the **SHORTCUT KEY** box as the macro will be assigned to a menu option.

(e) In the **STORE MACRO IN** box select the option **THIS WORKBOOK**.

(f) Enter a description of the macro in the Description box, eg, *'Prints the invoice'*.

(g) Click **OK** – you are now recording.

2   **Macro Recording.** Proceed as follows:

(a)   Check the printer is turned on.

(b) Select the options **FILE-PAGE SETUP** and select the **SHEET** tab.

(c) In the **PRINT AREA** box enter the cell range containing the invoice, eg **A1:K40** .

(d) Click **OK.**

(e) Select the option **FILE-PRINT**, check the various options and click **OK**.

(f) When printing is finished click the **STOP RECORDING** button (if you can't see it select **TOOLS-MACRO-STOP RECORDING**).

3   **Assigning the Macro to a Menu Option**. Click on the custom menu to open it and select the 'Print form' option. The Assign macro dialog box opens – select the macro **PRINT_INVOICE** and click **OK**. The macro is now assigned – test it.

Note: The Customize dialog box may need to be open while you are doing this.

4   Our second macro will be run from the menu option 'Clear form'; if a user starts keying in invoice details and then wishes to cancel the invoice this macro will automatically delete any information already entered. Again this macro is fairly straightforward; it is simply a matter of selecting all the possible data entry areas and then pressing the **DELETE** key. Proceed as follows:

(a) Select the options **TOOLS-MACRO-RECORD NEW MACRO**.

(b) The **RECORD MACRO** dialog box is displayed next; complete it as follows:

(c) Name the macro **Clear_Invoice.**

(d) Do not enter anything in the **SHORTCUT KEY** box as the macro will be assigned to a menu option.

(e) In the **STORE MACRO IN** box select the option **THIS WORKBOOK**.

(f) Enter a description of the macro in the Description box, eg, *'Clears the invoice'*.

(g) Click **OK** – you are now recording.

5 **Macro Recording.** Proceed as follows:

(a) Hold down the **CTRL** key and select the 10 customer detail fields (not the field names) – Invoice number, invoice date, contact name etc.

(b) Keep the **CTRL** key pressed down and select the range of cells holding the product details, eg cell range D24 to G33.

(c) Press the **DELETE** key on the keyboard.

(d) Click the **STOP RECORDING** button (if you can't see it select **TOOLS-MACRO-STOP RECORDING**).

6 Now assign the macro to the second menu option as before; to test it first fill in part of the invoice and run the macro from the menu – the contents should be cleared.

7 **Independent Task – Hiding and Displaying the Invoicing Menu**. Our final macro will hide the invoicing menu; unless it is hidden when not in use it will continue to be displayed irrespective of the workbook in use. In this situation using one of the menu options on another workbook would cause an error message to be displayed.This is a very simple macro to record so try it on your own; call the macro **Hide_Menu**. It is simply a matter of:

(a) recording the menu options **VIEW-TOOLBARS** and then de-selecting the Invoicing menu

(b) assigning the macro to the menu option and testing it (first you will have to re-display the invoicing menu)

Now try creating a macro that will automatically display the invoicing menu when the workbook is opened. You may need to refer back to the final task in the previous topic on how to do this. You can also create a macro that will automatically hide the menu when the workbook is closed.

Excel on the Web

Introduction

Excel and other Microsoft Office components are now so well integrated with Web-based technologies that the boundaries between them have become blurred. Excel lets you turn your worksheets and charts into Web pages; basically this means saving them in the standard Web page format – HTML. Having done this your Excel Web page can then be viewed using a Web browser such as Netscape or Internet Explorer. If you make your Excel Web page interactive then other users can change the data using Internet Explorer version 4.01 or later, if the Web page is made non-interactive then users can view the data but not change it.

Putting your Excel data on the Web has several advantages. It lets users access your worksheet data without needing Excel installed on their computers – all they need is a Web browser and access to the Web server where the pages are stored. You can also combine different types of data on a single Web page, from where it can be easily viewed or updated.

Different Microsoft components are necessary to create, view or modify Excel-based Web pages and to place them on a Web server; these are best checked out using the Help text – look up the term 'Web' in the Help index and then choose the topic 'Ways to put Microsoft Excel data on the Web'. For the purposes of this topic I assume that you have Internet Explorer, access to the Web and Web Query installed as part of Excel.

Topic Objectives

- To create and run a Web query.
- To create and edit a Web page in Excel.
- To use FrontPage Express to enhance an Excel Web page.
- To insert hyperlinks into a Web page.

Running a Web Query in Excel

1 **The Web Toolbar**. Open the **VIEW** menu, select **TOOLBARS** then **WEB**. The Web toolbar has similar buttons to a Web browser - Back, Forward, Stop etc. Clicking some of the buttons, eg 'Search the Web' or 'Home', simply calls up your Information Access Provider and/or starts your Web browser such as Internet Explorer.

2 **Opening an Excel workbook from a Web Browser**. Open Internet Explorer in offline mode. Open the **FILE** menu and select **OPEN**. Click the **BROWSE** button on the dialog box that appears and locate your Excel workbooks – you will need to alter the **FILES OF TYPE**: box to **ALL FILES** to view them.

Choose a workbook and select **OPEN** then **OK**. Internet Explorer opens an Excel window within the Explorer browser, allowing you to work with the workbook in the usual way. Close Internet Explorer now.

(3) **Running a Web Query**. Excel Query allows you to create a query for a particular Web site and download the results into an Excel workbook. This is particularly useful for rapidly changing information such as financial data. Once the data is downloaded to a workbook it can be analysed using the normal Excel features. We will try two of the sample sites and queries provided by Microsoft.

Open a new workbook and select the menu options **DATA-GET EXTERNAL DATA-RUN SAVED QUERY**. If the option is not available then you will need to install it from the Excel setup CD-ROM.

Select one of the Microsoft queries and click the **GET DATA** button. A dialog box asks you where you want to store the data, select **EXISTING WORKSHEET** and click **OK**.

If you are prompted to connect to your Internet Access Provider then do so.

(4) After a short delay the external data is downloaded into your workbook; check that the External Data toolbar is displayed, if not then select it using the **VIEW-TOOLBARS** command.

Click the **DATA RANGE PROPERTIES** button on the toolbar and a dialog box opens, offering various features, including how often you want the data refreshed or updated while you are connected to the Web site. Close the dialog box and toolbar and save the workbook as **Queries**.

(5) **Running a Dynamic Query.** The above query was a static query – it retrieves the same data each time it is run; to run a dynamic query you will need to specify the data.

Select cell **A1** of the second worksheet in your new workbook. Select the menu options **DATA-GET EXTERNAL DATA-RUN SAVED QUERY** as before. This time select the query **MICROSOFT INVESTOR STOCK QUOTES** and click the **GET DATA** button.

Select the default **EXISTING WORKSHEET** as before. You are now prompted to enter a stock fund as a parameter value. Enter MSFT for Microsoft and a stock quote for Microsoft will be downloaded into your worksheet.

Saving Excel Data as a Web Page

(1) **Previewing a Workbook as a Web Page**. Open the workbook **Book Sales**. Select the options **FILE-WEB PAGE PREVIEW**. A browser window opens, showing you how your worksheets, charts etc will look as a Web Page. You may well feel that as a Web page your workbook lacks visual impact; this is because Excel is not intended to be a fully featured Web page Editor, it is much more effective to create the basic Web page in Excel and then use another application to improve layout, formatting etc. For example Microsoft Word offers superior page editing features and of course a special purpose application such as Microsoft FrontPage (or the simpler version FrontPage Express included in Windows) is even better. In these applications you can modify your Web page, add text and graphics, and change the layout.

Another reason for using a Web page editor to enhance the basic Excel Web page is that many of the original Excel formats will be lost when it is saved as a Web page – refer to the appropriate Help text for a list of these.

2 **Creating a Web Page in Excel**. We will use the Workbook **Book Sales** as the basis for our Web page; make sure that the sheet containing the sales data is the active sheet.

(a) Select cells **A3** - **D8**, containing the first 5 months' data, including the row and column headings but excluding the title – see Figure 4.3 if necessary.

(b) Open the **FILE** menu and select **SAVE AS WEB PAGE**. When the dialog box appears alter the file name to **Book Sales Web Page** and click the **SELECTION** button to save only the selected cells.

(c) Click the **CHANGE TITLE** button and enter a suitable title. If you want the page to be amendable then select the **ADD INTERACTIVITY** box; however, the page may not display correctly unless you have Internet Explorer version 4.01 or later, plus the necessary Microsoft Office Web components. If in doubt do not select this box.

(d) Finally click the **PUBLISH** button. On the next dialog box check that the settings are correct and select the further option **OPEN PUBLISHED WEB PAGE IN BROWSER** if necessary.

(e) Click the **PUBLISH** button again and the worksheet cells are displayed as a Web page in the Internet Explorer browser. Close the browser.

3 **Adding Data to an Excel-based Web Page**. We now have a Web page containing a number of worksheet cells. We will add one of the charts from the **Book Sales** workbook to it. Select one of the graph sheets, eg the 3-D column chart and follow the following steps:

(a) Select the options **FILE-SAVE AS WEB PAGE**.

(b) On the **SAVE AS** dialog box click the **SELECTION** button to save only the chart; there is no need to add a title as the chart already has one.
Do not select the **ADD INTERACTIVITY** box, we do not want the chart to be modified except via the worksheet data.

(c) Amend the file name to **Book Sales Web Page** as before – this ensures that it will be saved on the same Web page as the cell data.

(d) Click the **PUBLISH** button. On the next dialog box check the name and path of the Web page and that the option **OPEN PUBLISHED WEB PAGE IN BROWSER** is selected.

(e) Click the **PUBLISH** button again. A dialog box may appear, reminding you that the Web page file **Book Sales Web Page** already exists and offering you the option of replacing it or adding to it. Take the option **ADD TO FILE**.

(f) The Web page opens in the browser; it now contains two elements, the worksheet cells and the 3-D chart. Close the browser.

Editing an Excel Web Page in Front Page Express

Microsoft FrontPage Express is a Web page editor included free with Windows and Internet Explorer from Windows 95 onwards. It is a cut-down version of Microsoft FrontPage. Similar in operation to a word processing or desktop publishing package it lets you create new Web pages or, as we will, edit an existing one. We will be briefly reviewing this application as a way of enhancing the basic Excel-based Web page; the instructions that follow are for the Windows 98 version, but earlier and later versions of FrontPage Express work in a similar way.

1   Click the Windows **START** button and select the options **PROGRAMS-INTERNET EXPLORER-FRONTPAGE EXPRESS**.

2   When the FrontPage Express window opens select **FILE-OPEN** then click the **BROWSE** button. Open the Web page that we have created in the previous task – **Book Sales Web Page**. The FrontPage Express editing screen is displayed now; in editing mode the Web page will obviously look different to the way it appears in a Web browser – we will review this later. In particular ignore the buttons marked with '?' and '!' symbols; these allow extra components to be entered and do not appear when viewed in the browser.

3   **Styles, Fonts and Colours.** These can be amended either using the Format toolbar or by right clicking the page item and selecting the appropriate Format option.

(a)   Select the title then right click it and select **FONT PROPERTIES**. Amend the font size, colour etc.

(b)   Right click a blank part of the page and use the **PAGE PROPERTIES** dialog box to alter the page background colour.

(c)   Right click the worksheet cells that appear on the page and use the **TABLE PROPERTIES** dialog box to alter the table colour, borders etc.

(d)   Right click the table again to change the **FONT PROPERTIES**.

     Notes: Use the **EDIT-UNDO** command (or button) to reverse unwanted changes. You can cut, copy, paste and format individual text in the usual way.

4   Save the above changes; leave your Web page open in FrontPage Express and carry on with the next task.

Viewing Your Web Page in a Browser

It is good idea when you are developing a Web page to have the Internet Explorer Web browser open as well as the FrontPage Express Web page editor. You can then 'flick' from one to the other to check the effects of changes. If your page is stored on a local drive or server then there is no need to be connected online.

1   Open Internet Explorer, if you are prompted to connect take the offline option.

Open the **FILE** menu and select **OPEN** – the Open dialogue box appears.
Click the **BROWSE** button then select the appropriate drive/folder and file name.
Click the **OPEN** button on both dialog boxes and your Web page is opened, ready for browsing.

(2) **Viewing the effects of changes.** Click the FrontPage Express and Explorer buttons on the taskbar; you are viewing the same file using two different applications.
Activate the FrontPage Express window.
Make a small change to the text of your Web page *without saving it*.
Activate the Explorer window and locate the text you have just changed – you will see that the change has not been updated in the browser application.
Activate the FrontPage Express window again and save the change now.
Activate the Explorer window again – the change is still not displayed.
Click the **REFRESH** button and Explorer will show the change.

(3) **Troubleshooting**: If changes made in edit mode (FrontPage Express) are not visible in browser mode (Internet Explorer) you have probably forgotten one of the two steps above – saving the change and clicking the Refresh button.
If you cannot edit or save a Web page then you are probably not in edit mode at all but browsing; this is a common mistake. You cannot edit any page – yours or someone else's – while you are browsing.

(4) For the next tasks you should have the Internet Explorer Web browser open as well as the FrontPage Express Web page editor.

115

Inserting Hyperlinks

(1) In FrontPage Express you can insert links to other web sites, pages on your own Web site, or simply to other parts of the same page. The links, ie what you click, can be text, icons or images. First we will insert a hyperlink to take you from the bottom to the top of the page. Microsoft calls intra-page links bookmarks; they are also referred to as anchors.
Make sure that you are viewing your home page in FrontPage Express not Explorer.

(2) **Inserting a Bookmark**. First we need to mark a place at the top of the page to serve as a bookmark.
Highlight the page title then open the **EDIT** menu and select **BOOKMARK** – a dialog box appears, showing the default bookmark name.
Click **OK** and you have created a bookmark – a named section of a Web page.

(3) **Inserting a Hyperlink**.

(a) Insert a blank line at the bottom of the page. On this new line type the text *Back to top* and then highlight it.

(b) Open the **INSERT** menu and select **HYPERLINK**.

(c) Click the **OPEN PAGES** tab in the dialog box that appears, make sure that your page is selected in the **OPEN PAGES** section.

(d) Now click the down arrow on the **BOOKMARK** section and select the bookmark you have just created. Click **OK**.

④ **Testing the Bookmark and Hyperlink**. First save the changes in FrontPage Express. Activate the Explorer window to browse your page and click the **REFRESH** button.
Now click the text **BACK TO TOP** and you are taken to the top of the page.

⑤ **Independent Task**. Activate the FrontPage Express window and create a bookmark and hyperlink that take you in the opposite direction, ie from the top to the bottom of the page.

Linking to a Web Page

In this task we will create a link between this Web page and a page on a Web site, but we could equally link to a page on the same drive/folder or Web server.

① Activate the FrontPage Express window and insert a blank line at a suitable place in your Web page.
Type the text 'Go to the .... Website' and then highlight it.
Take the menu options **INSERT-HYPERLINK-WORLD WIDE WEB**.

② Enter a suitable URL in the dialog box; remember to start with the prefix **http:**
If you wish you can also include a target frame. Click **OK**.

③ Save the changes in FrontPage Express and test the hyperlink in Internet Explorer, remembering to refresh the browser window. If it does not work correctly return to FrontPage Express and right click the hyperlink to edit it.

INDEX

117